Securing the System: Formal Methods for Error-Free Software

Naviya

Outline

Chapter 1

Introduction

Testing is a very important part of software development. Computer and software systems need to be tested before their final release to make sure they are free of errors. In general, making sure that a piece of software is free of bugs is an undecidable problem in computer science. However, there are two well-known methods for testing a software system to make sure a large class of errors are covered adequately. The first and primary type of method can be called *informal methods* which means that the software is examined with a comprehensive set of test cases. Although this type of method is simple and can recognize many errors easily, it cannot guarantee that the system is free of bugs. A second method, which we focus on here, is called *formal methods*. In contrast to the first type, formal methods can be used to verify and prove that a piece of software is free of errors based on a given model. We focus on methods involving verification. The main types of formal verification include *model checking* and *theorem proving*. In model checking, the system is defined by a set of states and a set of transitions between them. Also, properties are considered about the system and shown to be true or false. Often a model of the system is defined based on a transition graph [13]. This graph is called a Kripke structure or state-transition graph. Each node in the graph represents a state of the system being modeled and each edge stands for a transition from a source to a destination state. On the other hand, in theorem proving, models can be defined based on sets of features usually expressed as mathematical definitions, and theorems stated and proved that verify the model and the features. While theorem provers can provide proofs for general cases and arbitrary values, model checkers are more automatic but not as general and often must rely on special values and cases. Model checkers can find counterexamples for a property but theorem provers cannot. In theorem proving, we can either prove a property or fail to prove it. Failing can be because of the proof approach, incorrect assumptions, or incorrect statement of the property. Finding counterexamples is not useful in our approach; instead an unsuccessful branch in a proof can provide information about the reason for failure and help us determine how to correct it, and successful proofs can give us hints about how to prove similar properties in the future. This is not true about the model checking, where successful proofs are transparent to the user and cannot be exploited. Formal verification has been taken more seriously since the mid-90s because of some significant failures in industry, such as the recall of the Intel Pentium 5 due to an error in the division algorithm for floating point numbers [75]. Verification of software, hardware, and systems is improving rapidly and it now plays an important role in many applications such as security, medicine, etc. Verification of medical systems is vital because the life of patients often depends on it. A buggy medical system is dangerous for patients, and can lead to distress for doctors and nurses when they follow the wrong advice.

In recent decades, interactive theorem provers have been applied to a variety of large case studies in two distinct domains. The first one is programs and systems verification and the second one is formalization of large mathematical proofs. A notable example of the first one is the CompCert project [55], which is a fully verified compiler for a large subset of the C programming language. The formal proof is done using the Coq proof assistant [8, 15] and it guarantees that a compiled program behaves exactly as determined by the original source program according to the semantics of the C language. Another noteworthy example in this category is the verification of the Sel4 operating system in the theorem prover Isabelle/HOL [56]. As for the second category, two large examples of completely formalized mathematical results include the Feit-Thompson theorem in algebraic group theory verified in Coq [40] and the Kepler conjecture in the HOL Light and Isabelle/HOL theorem provers [43].

A more recent application of formal verification is in the field of systems biology. Indeed, formal verification of biological systems turns out to be very useful, e.g., [39]. The main reason is that biologists want to validate/refute hypotheses on their biological systems before testing them on real systems. This often means that the model of their system should be verified. Many biological systems can be modelled as graphs whose nodes represent all different possible configurations of the system and whose edges encode meaningful configuration changes. It is then possible to define and prove properties concerning the temporal evolution of the biological species involved in the system [30, 73]. This allows deep insights into the biological system at issue, in particular concerning the biological transitions governing it, and the reactions the system have when confronted with external factors such as disease, medicine, and environmental changes [24, 79]. By understanding and proving properties of a biological system, there is a higher chance of treating diseases and developing medicines that remedy them. Furthermore, weak points of the system can be detected and better prevention against disease and other external problems can be proposed. Finally, biological system recovery after damage has occurred can be studied and verified. In summary, behavior, disease, effects of medicine, external problems, environmental change impacts, and system recovery of a biological system can all be detected and verified using formal verification. Biological systems can be anything from a single cell in an organ to the whole body of a live creature. The biological entities we are going to implement and verify are parts of the human neural network.

In the last decades, there has been much promising research in the field of formal modelling and verification of biological systems. As far as the modelling of biological systems is concerned, in the literature we can find both qualitative and quantitative approaches. To express the qualitative nature of dynamics, the most used formalisms are Thomas discrete models [82], Petri nets [70], π-calculus [72], bio-ambients [71], and reaction rules [10]. To capture the dynamics from a quantitative point of view, ordinary or stochastic differential equations are used extensively. More recent approaches include hybrid Petri nets [47] and hybrid automata [2], stochastic π-calculus [67], and rule-based languages with continuous/stochastic dynamics such as Kappa [18]. Relevant properties concerning the obtained models are then often expressed using a formalism called *temporal logic* [54] and verified thanks to model checkers such as NuSMV [12] or PRISM [51]. In [21], the authors propose the use of modal linear logic as a unified framework to encode both biological systems and temporal properties of their dynamic behavior. They focus on a model of the P53/Mdm2 DNA-damage repair mechanism and they prove some desired properties using the Coq Proof Assistant, with the help of a Lambda Prolog prover [62]. In [28], the Coq Proof Assistant is exploited to prove two theorems linking the topology and the dynamics of gene regulatory networks. In [69], the authors advocate the use of higher-order logic to formalize reaction kinetics and exploit the HOL Light theorem prover to verify some reaction-based models of biological networks. The Porgy system is introduced in [4]. It is a visual environment, which allows the modelling of biochemical systems as rule-based models. Rewriting strategies are used to choose the rules to be applied. In [53], the authors simulate and model Biochemical reaction networks as abstract models of molecular processes in well-mixed solutions. They show that using the theorem prover Isabelle/HOL [64] can give more generality in comparison to the model checker PRISM [51].

In the recent years, much attention has been directed towards the study of the structure and the functional behavior of brain networks. The *Connectome* project [76, 77, 78] mainly focuses on macro scales and is based on diffusion or functional MRI data [35], although it claims that it does graph analysis on both micro and macro scales. This project does not use formal verification but it is mainly based on large scale simulations. Here, we want to promote a more fundamental and formal approach to the study of specific neuronal micro-circuits. In the literature, this is not the only attempt to investigate neural networks. As far as human neural networks are concerned, there is recent work that has focused on their formal verification. In [26, 27], the synchronous paradigm has been exploited to model neurons and some small neuronal circuits with a relevant topological structure and behavior and to prove some properties concerning their dynamics. Our approach is based on the use of the Coq proof assistant, which to the best of our knowledge is the first approach to employ a proof assistant, is more general. As a matter of fact, we guarantee that the properties we prove are true in the general case, such as true for any input values, any length of input, and any amount of time.

In this project, we exploit some techniques of software verification to verify the dynamic behavior of biological human neural networks. There are three major steps in our model. We start with the smallest unit of human neural networks which are neurons. We define neurons as the base of our model and verify some properties of them. As mentioned above in [26, 27], the authors consider the synchronous paradigm to model and verify some specific graphs constituted by a small number of biological neurons. These graphs or mini-circuits, characterized by biologically relevant structures and behaviors, are referred to as *archetypes* and constitute the fundamental elements of neuronal information processing. Archetypes are the second step in our model. They represent basic functional structures of neural networks. Rhythmic motions such as walking, running, breathing, etc. are well-known examples of actions that are generated by composition of archetypes in our neural network. These actions are controlled by particular neuronal circuits called Central Generator Patterns (CGP) [60]. These CGPs have the ability to create oscillatory activities under various conditions. We will explain archetypes in the next chapter in more detail.

Archetypes can be coupled to constitute the elementary building blocks of bigger neuronal circuits. For this reason, their study has become an emerging question in the domain of neuro-sciences, especially for their potential integration with neuro-computational techniques [59]. Furthermore, understanding these micro-circuits can help in detecting weakly active or inactive zones of the human brain, and in identifying networks whose role is crucial in performing various vital activities, such as breathing or moving, as mentioned above. The third step in our model is composition of archetypes. In this book, we use the terms *composition* and *coupling* of archetypes interchangeably. Composition of archetypes can generate more complicated functions. When archetypes are coupled together, they can perform more complex actions but if a composition does not introduce a new behaviour, then the coupling is equivalent to an already known archetype. We define and prove some properties about composition of archetypes in our model.

In the work proposed in [26, 27], some model checkers such as Lesar [44] and Kind2 [42] are employed to automatically verify properties concerning the dynamics of neurons, six basic archetypes and their coupling. However, model checkers prove properties for some given parameter intervals, and do not handle inputs of arbitrary length. In our work, we use the Coq Proof Assistant to model part of human neural networks and prove some important properties about neurons, archetypes, and their composition. In terms of theorem proving, there is a large variety of automated and interactive theorem provers [34, 45]. Less expressive logics can be automated easier while more expressive logics provide more flexibility in defining models and proving their properties. Coq implements a highly expressive higher-order logic called the Calculus of Inductive Constructions [8] in which we can directly introduce datatypes modelling neurons and archetypes, their couplings, and express properties about them. Coq is a widely used system that won the prestigious ACM Software System Award in 2013. Other theorem provers in this category include Nuprl [14], the PVS specification and Verification System [65], and Isabelle/HOL [64].

Implementation of our model does not depend on advanced features of Coq like dependent types or the hierarchy of universes, and thus while we take into account everything about the model and properties, our model is not difficult to understand, even for readers with a basic knowledge of theorem proving, and could likely be translated fairly easily to other interactive theorem provers such as those mentioned above. Some of Coq's features that were most useful in our work include its general facilities for defining datatypes, which we used to directly model neurons, archetypes, and their composition, its powerful mechanisms for carrying out proofs by structural induction and case analysis, and its standard libraries that helped in reasoning about rational numbers and functions on them. One of the main advantages of using Coq for our purposes is the generality of its proofs; Coq is a theorem prover and as mentioned before theorem provers can be used to prove properties about arbitrary values of parameters, such as any length, any input sequence, or any number of neurons. Of course, in any verification effort, whether model checking or theorem proving, the guarantees provided rely on the correctness of any assumptions made; in our setting, this means that we must do our best to correctly model neurons and archetypes. These are some of the main reasons that we choose Coq for the verification of our model.

The goal of this project is to provide a model of crucial neuronal networks that is as complete as possible. With model checking, we have to give particular values for various quantities, such as number of neurons, and different parameters for each neuron. We could apply this to a particular patient by inputting the specific values for the specific patient. When stating a property in theorem prover, it is generally a universally quantified implication, where the quantification is over quantities such as number of neurons and values of other parameters. The implication contains all the assumptions on the left and the conclusion on the right. The property applies to all patients. It can be instantiated by providing the quantities for a particular patient or class of patients, and if all the assumptions hold for this patient, then the conclusion holds as well. One of the main motivations for modeling such a system is to make the assumptions clear so that these assumptions can be tested in real life.

The long-term goal of this project it to obtain a model for a big part of the human neural network. We believe the approach introduced in this project for neural networks is very promising because our model can be generalized to the verification of other kinds of biological networks, such as gene regulatory, metabolic, or environmental networks. The reason is that other biological networks have the same structure, which includes biological entities having interactions via some form of connections between them.

1.1 Contributions

- Significant steps toward a formal model for biological systems:
  Most biological models focus on a particular part or organ of a body. Here, we provide a formal model for neuronal networks, which is general enough to extend to a big part of the

human neural network and to other kinds of networks in the human body, such as gene regulatory networks.

- Showed that theorem proving can be used to formulate such a model, which allows more generality and flexibility in proving properties:

  Most biological frameworks use model checkers to have the benefit of automatic verification but they rely on special cases and values for properties. Our model is formalized in the Coq proof assistant, which is a theorem prover, that allows us to prove properties for any cases, and arbitrary values and input length.

- Structural model that can be extended easily:

  In our model, we start from modeling and proving properties about neurons, which are the smallest unit of neural networks. Then, we focus on functional structures consisting of two or more neurons, which are called archetypes. Finally, we model archetype compositions which represent more complicated functions in the human neural network. A possible future goal is to extend our model to some crucial neural network involved in important human functions. Our model is designed to be extensible in the sense that we can add and prove more properties about neurons, archetypes, or more sophisticated networks.

- Proved six properties about neurons, two properties about archetypes and two properties about composition of archetypes:

  All but one of these properties are formalized in Coq and our contribution includes a more general and complete set of properties than model checking approaches. We have discussed the properties that we consider here with biologists, and confirmed that they do indeed have applications in biology [41, 68]. We also model some other archetypes and compositions for which properties about them can be defined and proved as future work. To be more precise, we both proved mathematically and verified in Coq Properties 1 to 5, 7 to 9, 14, and 15. We also proved Property 6 mathematically. The rest of properties are stated mathematically and in Coq but their proofs are left for future work.

We published a paper [5], which includes our research on modelling and verifying four basic properties of neural networks in Coq. We also published a more extended article [20] which includes the model checking method, our theorem proving approach, and their comparison. We also published a book chapter [22] about the application of our logical approach in bio-medicine and neuroscience.

The rest of the book is organized as follows. In Chapter 2, we introduce the state of the art relative to neural network modelling and neural network generations. We also describe the computational model we have chosen, the Leaky Integrate and Fire model, and we briefly introduce some basic archetypes. In Chapter 3, we present the Coq proof assistant, its basic data types, inductive data types, functions, and proof tactics. In Chapter 4, we present our model of neural networks in Coq, which includes definitions of neurons, operations on them, and useful functions for expressing behavior of neurons. In Chapter 5, we present and discuss important properties, starting with properties of single input neurons. We present and prove five properties about single input neurons in this chapter. We also state and prove a property about multiple input neurons. We finish this chapter by presenting the statements of these properties in Coq and we show one Coq proof for illustration. In Chapter 6, we present archetypes definitions in Coq. We introduce the statement of four important archetypes and some properties about them. We also present the proofs of two properties about one of these archetypes in this chapter. In Chapter 7, we introduce two possible compositions of archetypes. We also state two properties about one of these compositions and present their proof. Finally, in Chapter 8, we conclude and discuss future work. The accompanying Coq code can be found.

Chapter 2

Background

In this book, we use formal modelling and verification to build a model of neural networks and prove some properties of them. Based on this model, we can provide proofs of properties about functioning and malfunctioning of neural networks in different cases. To achieve this goal, we employ the Coq proof assistant and we model and verify neurons, archetypes, and composition of archetypes. We start with reviewing previous research in the area of biological networks in systems biology.

2.1 State of the Art on Formal Modelling and Verification of Biological Networks

In systems biology, biological systems are often modelled as biological networks. In this section, we mainly focus on biological networks but when we want to refer to a biological system, we say it explicitly. Several kinds of biological networks are in the scope of systems biology. Here, we are going to enumerate five of them, which are very common in the literature, e.g., [19]. The first type of networks is gene regulatory networks, which represent genes, their regulators, and the regulatory relationships between them. The second type of networks is protein-protein interaction networks, which model the physical contacts between proteins in a cell. The third type of biological networks is metabolic networks, that represent the biochemical reactions catalyzed by enzymes in a cell. The fourth type of biological networks is ecological networks, which model the biological interactions of an ecosystem. The fifth type of biological networks we mention here and this book is focused on is biological neural networks, which describe how neurons in the brain communicate through their synapses. These are just some examples of crucial biological networks in the field of systems biology. Certainly, there are more in this field that are explored or to be explored but, in this section, we focus on some of the aforementioned networks, in particular, on biological neural networks.

As mentioned in the introduction, there are two major approaches for modelling and verification of biological networks, which are quantitative, and qualitative. While qualitative methods are conceptual (e.g. they model the presence or absence of a biological entity) such as spikes in the output of a neuron, quantitative methods aim at counting, measuring, and expressing data using numbers such as measuring an enzyme level in an organ or expressing the speed rate of a reaction. We enumerated some examples of both categories in the introduction. Here, we are going to give a brief explanation for some of them in each category. Petri nets [70] fall into the category of qualitative methods. Petri nets represent bipartite directed graphs which have two types of nodes, namely resources and transitions. Transitions correspond to events that alter resources of the system. Thomas' discrete model or Thomas' regulatory networks is another type of qualitative approach, which are represented as regulatory graphs where nodes are regulatory components such as genes or proteins, and two types of edges namely positive and negative, which show activation and inhibition respectively [82]. We use the same kind of edges for inputs of a neuron, which will be explained later. Another qualitative form of modelling is reaction rules-based modelling [10]. There are rule-based languages that model biochemical reactions by defining a set of reactants that can be transformed to a set of products according to some rate laws [10]. We introduce briefly some tools and languages for reaction rules-based modelling later. π-calculus [72] and bio-ambients [71] are two well-known examples of process algebras, which is another major form of qualitative modelling. Process algebras can model biological entities as abstract processes that can interact with each other and reactions of these entities can be modelled as actions. π-calculus is the most common process algebra used in systems biology in which there are complementary channels identified by names for process communications. Bio-ambients allow the modelling of physically bounded compartments that contain processes communicating between them. Pure logic is also used as a qualitative approach, which we use in this project. As mentioned in the introduction, this method is based on creating a model in some logic and verifying the model and properties according to the inference rules of that logic.

We do not use a quantitative approach in this book, but we explain briefly some of the methods in this category, which we mentioned in the introduction section. The most common and classical method is using ordinary or stochastic differential equations, where interactions between system components are implemented by sigmoid expressions embedded in differential equations. Another quantitative approach, Hybrid Petri nets [47], considers two types of states and transitions, which are discrete and continuous. Hybrid Petri nets are well-suited for modelling biological pathways as hybrid systems with both discrete and continuous evolutions. Timed automata [58] are finite state automata extended with time constraints. They are another quantitative method in which the amount of time spent in particular states is limited and transitions are enabled within some time intervals. Hybrid automata [2] combine finite state automata with continuously evolving variables. Both timed and hybrid automata are well-suited for modelling time related aspects of biological networks such as duration of activities. Although, our approach in this project is not a quantitative one, time plays a very important role in our model, which will be explained later in this chapter. The other well-known quantitative method is stochastic process algebras, which are process algebra models adorned with quantitative information to produce stochastic processes. The most exploited methodology in this area is stochastic π-calculus [67] where each channel has a stochastic rate and is associated with process algebras that specify complicated kinetic formulas. The last quantitative method we enumerate here is rule-based languages with continuous/stochastic dynamics such as Kappa [18]. Rules in these languages are associated with continuous or stochastic dynamics. In Kappa, rules fire stochastically according to standard continuous time Monte Carlo algorithms. We have just mentioned some of the well-known qualitative and quantitative approaches in the area of formal modelling and verification. In [19], these methods are explained in more detail.

One leading platform for modelling biological systems is the Biochemical Abstract Machine (BIOCHAM) [31]. BIOCHAM is a software environment for modeling and analyzing biochemical systems. BIOCHAM contains four main components, which are a rule-based language for modelling biochemical systems, different types of simulators, a temporal logic-based language to formalize temporal properties of a biological system and validate models according to some specifications, and unique features for developing, correcting, reducing, and coupling models of biological systems. These systems can be as simple as a particular reaction in an organ or a cell or as complex as a whole body of a live creature. BIOCHAM is a free and open source system and is available online . Another leading platform for modelling biological systems in BioNetGen [9, 29] which is able to specify and simulate rule-based models of biochemical systems such as signal transudation, metabolic, and genetic regulatory networks. BioNetGen provides both textual and graphical formats.

There are several languages for modeling biochemical and biological networks. The most common representation format is called the Systems Biology Markup Language (SBML [48], which is an XML based representation format for expressing computational models of biological processes such as cell signal pathways, regulatory networks, metabolic networks, etc. SMBL is documented at http://sbml.org and it is considered as a standard for expressing models of biological systems among biologists and biochemists. that are compatible with SMBL. Another common language is the Systems Biology Graphical Notation (SBGN [74]. This software is a standard for graphical representation of biological systems. It has the same capability as SBML for expressing regulatory and metabolic networks and other biological processes, but graphically in this case. BIOCHAM and BioNetGen are compatible with both SMBL and SBGN.

Note that BIOCHAM, SMBL, BioNetGen, and SBGN are platforms or languages; they are not models. As mentioned earlier, most research in the area of building a model for biological systems is restricted to a particular organ, application, or biological process. Some of these models are more general than others, but they cannot be considered a general model for the whole body. In this book, we move one step forward toward creating a general model for the human neural network by modeling the neural networks basic functional structures. Our formal model for biological networks can be generalized to other kinds of networks. We are going to list some research that has been done in this area in the rest of this section.

In the area of biological systems, most research is focused on a special organ or part of a human body or other living creature. In [10], the authors introduce a formalism to represent molecular biology networks at the protein interaction level. They analyze both protein-protein and protein-DNA interaction networks. They formalize a model for molecular cell cycles in mammals. They build their model as an extension of the cell cycle control reaction network by Kohn [50]. In their model, they use temporal logic to express properties of the system and model checking to verify them. In similar research [30], the authors give a comprehensive introduction of modelling an environment for biological networks and biochemical processes in BIOCHAM.

In [24], the authors put several biological systems together all modelled in BIOCHAM using temporal logic constraints. They design, optimize, and predict a coupled model of the mammalian cell cycle, circadian clock, DNA repair system, and Irinotecan metabolism and exposure control; each system is described in more detail below. Their research can be considered a survey of previous research on different biological systems starting with one of the most common ones, which is the mammalian cell cycle. Some key genes and proteins display some sustained oscillations with a period of approximately 24 hours. A biochemical clock in each cell is responsible for working in this circadian manner, which is the next modelled system in their research. As mentioned earlier in [26, 27], the authors present a model for a DNA repair mechanism that works based on two proteins called P53 and Mdm2 using the Coq proof assistant. In [24], they express this system but in BIOCHAM. The last model in this article is about metabolism and exposure control of an anticancer medicine called Irinotecan. There are substances called Camptothecins that are extractable from Chinese trees and can be used as a treatment for digestive cancers. Because these substances are toxic, some semi-synthetic water-soluble derivative of Camptothecins such as Irinotecan are used instead. The article brings all these models together in a coupled model whose key properties are expressed in temporal logic.

A notable portion of research in the area of verification of biological networks is dedicated to Biological Regulatory Networks (BRN) or gene regulatory networks. These two are usually used interchangeably and they are defined as a collection of biological entities or molecular regulators that interact with each other and other substances in a cell to specify the task of the cell. In general, there are two types of modelling of these networks, which are synchronous and asynchronous [36]. In a synchronous model, expression levels of several genes are changed simultaneously in consecutive time points while in an asynchronous model, all genes take different amounts of time to make a transition, which can be more complicated to model and analyze. An asynchronous model based on Boolean formalization, is proposed by Rene Thomas [80]. Later, he proposed a model based on asynchronous automata [81]. His model is studied in detail in [7] by employing temporal logic and verifying the model using model checking. A review of dynamic models of gene regulatory networks from experimental data using computational methods is given in [46]. Also, a formal semantics of BRN in terms of transition systems, which is well-suited for model checking, is presented in [6]. This field of research in verification of biological networks is still an area to explore further, especially by using proof assistants in addition to model checkers.

There are other networks that are similar to human neural networks or BRN and modelling them can move us toward modelling more complicated biological structures. As mentioned earlier, Porgy [32] is one of these modelling frameworks that is employed in [4] for exploring rule-based models of biochemical systems. Other types of networks can be explored using rule-base models and algebraic methods. The authors of [32] and others also implement an algebraic method based on labelled-graph strategic rewriting in Porgy for analyzing network generations and propagation mechanisms of social networks [33].

To verify a model, there are two major requirements. First, the model and its expected properties should be defined based on some logic or formalism. Using different logics for expressing and proving properties of biological networks is another area of research, which is explored as well. For instance, hybrid linear logic [38] is introduced for constrained transition systems with applications to molecular biology in [11]. Second, the model should be verified using some tools. Most research in this area uses model checkers to verify their model because it is simple and automatic. Model checkers lack generality and usually they cannot verify a model for arbitrary length of inputs and outputs, but only some research uses theorem provers. Theorem provers are more manual but they are more general and can provide proofs for any length of inputs and outputs; for example, recall that the Coq proof assistant implements higher-order logic. In our model, we use first-order logic, where the terms include the data structures of Coq such as lists, and proofs include structural induction over these data types. As mentioned earlier, we keep our model simple, which allows it to be easily translated to other theorem provers. The first step here is to better recognize the structure and the dynamics of neural networks. In the next section, we present three generations of models for human neural networks and in the following section after that, we explain the model we choose in detail.

2.2 Neural Network Model Generations

In the literature, it is possible to distinguish three generations of human neural network models [57, 66]. First generation models are identified with the one introduced by McCulloch-Pitts [61]. This model is based on discrete inputs and outputs. Computational units have a set of logical gates. Also, neurons work with a staircase threshold activation function. In other words, a neuron receives some binary inputs, each input has a weight, and if the weighted sum of inputs is greater than or equal to the threshold, the output will be one (spike emission), otherwise it will be zero (no spike emission). This model is obsolete now. It is not able to deal with many cases including very simple ones such as the XOR function [63].

In the second generation models, neuron behaviours are governed by real valued functions. Even their output values are real, although they can be rounded to zero or one depending on the application. Most common real-valued functions for this model are sigmoid and hyperbolic tangent. The most well-known network based on this model is the multilayer perceptron [17]. This kind of model is a very good fit for artificial neural networks. It is widely used in the field of machine learning, automatic classification, and clustering.

In this book, we consider third generation models of neural networks. They are known as *spiking neural networks* [66] and have been proposed in the literature with different complexities and capabilities. They are characterized by the relevance of time aspects. In this work, we focus on the Leaky Integrate and Fire (LI&F) model originally proposed in [52]. We will explain this model in detail later. This model is a computationally efficient approximation of a single-compartment model [49] and is abstract enough to allow the application of formal verification techniques. In such a model, neurons integrate present and past inputs in order to update their membrane potential values. Whenever the potential exceeds a given threshold, an output signal is fired.

As far as spiking neural networks are concerned, in the literature there are a few attempts at giving formal models for them. In [3], a mapping of spiking neural P systems into timed automata is proposed. A P system is a computational model that performs calculations using a biologically inspired process. In that work, the dynamics of neurons are expressed in terms of evolution rules and durations are given in terms of the number of rules applied. Timed automata are also exploited in [23] to model LI&F networks. This modelling is substantially different from the one proposed in [3] because an explicit notion of duration of activities is given. Such a model is formally validated against some crucial properties defined as temporal logic formulas and is then exploited to find an assignment for the synaptic weights of neural networks so that they can reproduce a given behaviour.

Another recent application of formal methods in computer science to neuro-sciences is given in [26, 27], where the authors model LI&F neurons and some basic small circuits using the synchronous language Lustre. Such a language is dedicated to the modelling of reactive systems, i.e., systems which constantly interact with the environment and which may have an infinite duration. It relies on the notion of logical time: time is considered as a sequence of discrete instants, and an instant is a point in time where external input events can be observed, computations can be done, and outputs can be emitted. Lustre is used not only to encode neurons and some basic archetypes (simple series, parallel composition, etc, but also some properties concerning their dynamic evolution. Some model checkers such as Lesar and Kind2 are then employed to automatically prove these properties for some given parameter intervals. This research is the most related research to the research in this book. In fact, we build our model as an extension to the model proposed in [26, 27], but instead of model checkers, we verify properties of neurons and archetypes using theorem proving in the Coq proof assistant. Our work directly expands the work done in Lustre. As mentioned earlier, theorem proving provides us generality in comparison to model checkers. For example, authors set parameters of neurons such as leak factor and activation threshold (explained in the next section to specific values. They also multiply these values by 10 to avoid dealing with real values because the model checking takes too long with real values. They also set the length of the input (e.g. the number of neurons of a single series to small values such as 5 or 6. In our model, the length of the input can be arbitrarily large and we do not set the parameters of neurons or archetypes to specific values. They are real values in the given range of the LI&F model. The journal paper we published [20] is a survey on both approaches to the verification of neuronal networks.

LI&F networks extended with probabilities are formalized as discrete-time Markov chains in [25]. The proposed framework is then exploited to introduce an algorithm which reduces the number of neurons and synaptic connections of input networks while preserving their dynamics.

2.3 The Leaky Integrate and Fire Model

Neurons are the smallest unit of a neural network [68]. They are basically just a single cell. We can consider them simply as a function with one or more inputs and a single output. A human neuron receives its inputs via its *dendrites*. Dendrites are short extensions connected to the neuron body, which is called the *soma*. Inputs are provided in the form of electrical pulses (spikes For each neuron there is another extension, called the *axon*, which plays the role of output. This extension is also connected to the cell body, but it is longer than the dendrites. Each neuron has its own activation threshold, which is coded somehow inside the soma. The *membrane potential* of a neuron, representing the difference of electrical potential across the cell membrane, depends on the spikes received through the ingoing dendrites. Both current and past spikes are taken into account, even if old spikes contribution is lower. In particular, the *leak factor* weakens past spikes. When the membrane potential of a neuron passes its threshold, the neuron fires a spike in the axon. Neurons can be connected to other neurons.

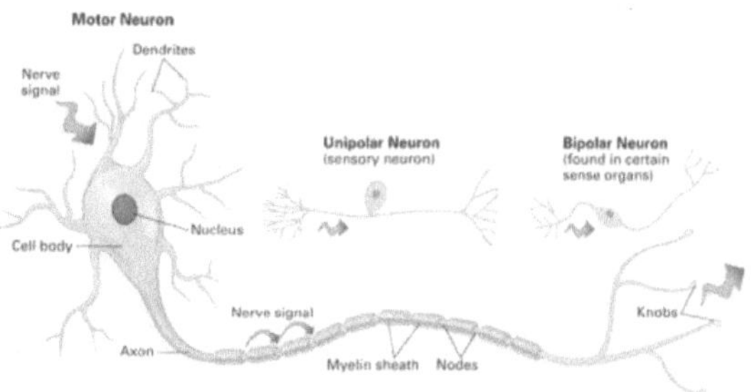

Figure 1. Structure of a neuron [1]

Connections happen between the axon of a neuron and a dendrite of another neuron. Theses connections are called *synaptic connections* and the location of the connection is called a *synapse*. They are responsible for transmitting signals between neurons. The structure of a neuron is shown in Figure 1.

The smallest unit after a neuron is an archetype. An archetype is a functional structure which consists of two or more neurons. We can say that neurons are like letters of a given alphabet and archetypes can be seen as syllables of the alphabet. When we compose syllables, we can either obtain existing words or not. Six sample archetypes are shown in Figure 2. Some properties about these archetypes have been verified using the model checkers Lesar and Kind2 in [26, 27]. In Figure 2, S and the S_is represent neurons, each incoming edge to a neuron shows an input of that neuron, and each outgoing edge is the neuron output. When there is more than one outgoing edge, it means the neuron sends its only output to different destinations. Recall that neurons have only one output. A filled black circle at the end of an input of a neuron shows that the input acts as an *inhibitor* for the neuron. When there is no black circle for an input of a neuron, the input acts as an *activator* for the neuron. We will explain later how inhibitors and activators can be modelled using negative and positive weights respectively. Note that in Figure 2 (a), (b), and (c), the number of neurons, which is denoted by n, can be arbitrarily large. As mentioned in the previous chapter, archetypes can be coupled to constitute the elementary building blocks of bigger neuronal circuits, but first we need to have a model for neurons and neuronal archetypes.

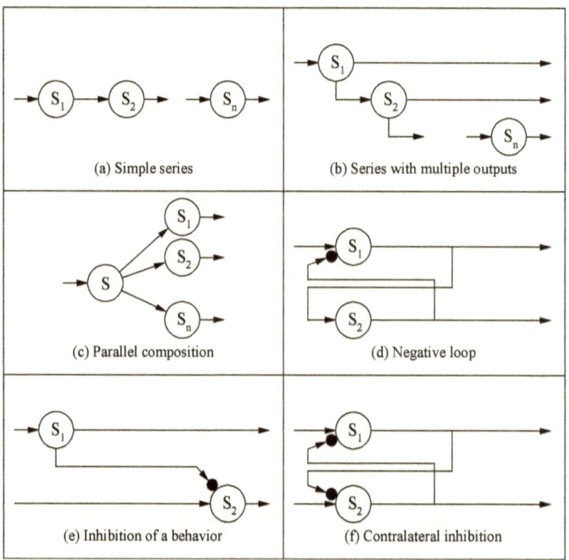

Figure 2. Six important archetypes [26, 27]

More formally, the following definition can be given for networks of LI&F neurons, adopted from [37, 52].

Definition 1 (LI&F Neural Network). *A LI&F Neural Network is a tuple* (V, E, w)*, where:*

- V *is the set of LI&F neurons,*
- $E \subseteq V \times V$ *is the set of synapses,*
- $w: E \rightarrow \mathbb{Q} \cap [-1,1]$ *is the synapse weight function associating a weight* $w_{u,v}$ *to each synapse* (u, v)*.*

We distinguish three disjoint sets of neurons: V_i *(input neurons),* V_{int} *(intermediary neurons), and* V_o *(output neurons), with* $V = V_i \cup V_{int} \cup V_o$*.*

A LI&F neuron *is characterized by a tuple* (τ, r, p, y)*, where:*

- $\tau \in \mathbb{Q}^+$ *is the* firing threshold *or* activation threshold,

- $r \in \mathbb{Q} \cap [0, 1]$ *is the* leak factor,

- $p\colon \mathbb{N} \to \mathbb{Q}$ *is the [membrane]* potential *function defined as:*

$$p(t) = \begin{cases} \sum_{i=1}^{m} w_i.x_i(t), & \text{if } p(t-1) \geq \tau \\ \sum_{i=1}^{m} w_i.x_i(t) + r \cdot p(t-1), & \text{if } p(t-1) < \tau \end{cases} \tag{1}$$

with $p(0) = 0$ and where $x_i(t) \in \{0, 1\}$ is the signal received at the time t by the neuron through its ith output of m input synapses (observe that the past potential is multiplied by the leak factor while current inputs are not weakened),

- $y\colon \mathbb{N} \to \{0, 1\}$ *is the neuron output function, defined as:*

$$y(t) = \begin{cases} 1 & \text{if } p(t) \geq \tau \\ 0 & \text{if } p(t) < \tau \end{cases} \tag{2}$$

The set of neurons of a LI&F neural network can be divided into input, intermediary, and output neurons as mentioned above. Each input neuron can only receive external signals as input and the output of each output neuron is considered as an output for the network. Output neurons are the only ones whose output is not connected to other neurons.

Chapter 3

The Coq Proof Assistant

In this chapter, we present the basic elements of Coq that we use to represent our model and prove properties about it. More complete documentation of Coq can be found in [8, 15]. Coq is a proof assistant that implements the Calculus of Inductive Constructions [16], which is an expressive higher-order logic. Using this software, we can express and prove properties in this logic. Expressions in the logic include a functional programming language. It is a typed language, which means that every Coq expression has a type. The most basic types in Coq are `Set` and `Prop`. `Set` is the type of data in Coq, while `Prop` is the type of formulas, which appears in theorems and lemmas, described below. Other types in Coq can be defined as elements of `Set` and `Prop`. In other words, whenever we need to define a new data type, we must use `Set` and when we need to define a formula, we must use `Prop`. A formula can be as simple as `True` or `False` or can be a complicated property that needs to be proved.

Coq provides a facility for defining inductive types. Inductive types are made from one or more base cases and some inductive cases. For example, natural numbers in Coq are defined as follows: `0` is a natural number. Also, every number that is a successor of another natural number is a natural number. The inductive definition of natural numbers is shown in Figure 3. Note that the general structure of a definition is displayed using a blue background and a piece of Coq code is displayed using an orange background in the figures of this chapter. Successor of `n` is denoted by `S n` which is equal to `n + 1`. Here `0` is the constructor for the base case and `S` is the constructor for the inductive case. The type of `S` is `nat -> nat`; it takes a natural number as an argument and constructs its successor. With this definition, we can build all natural numbers. For example, `4 = S 3 = S (S 2) = S (S (S 1)) = S (S (S (S 0)))`.

```
Inductive nat : Set :=
  | O : nat
  | S : nat -> nat.
```

Figure 3. Inductive definition of natural numbers in Coq

Another inductive type in Coq is `list`. A list can be empty or it can consist of a head and a tail. The head is the first element in the list and the tail is the rest of the elements in the list. The tail of a list is a list itself, while the head of a list has the same type as all the other elements in the list. In the inductive definition of `list` shown in Figure 4, A represents the type of the elements in the list and can be instantiated with any type. For example, `list nat` is the type for lists of natural numbers. `nil` denotes an empty list of type A for any A. `[]` is another notation for an empty list. `cons x l` takes an argument of type A such as `x` and a list of type A such as `l`, and constructs a list with `x` as head and `l` as tail. Thus, the type of cons is A $\rightarrow$ `list` A $\rightarrow$ `list` A, as shown in Figure 4.

```
Inductive list (A: Type) : Type :=
 | nil : list A
 | cons : A -> list A -> list A.
```

Figure 4. Inductive definition of lists in Coq

The type of elements of a list can be omitted sometimes because it can be inferred by Coq. For example, if `l` is the list `(cons 3 nil)`, then Coq will infer that A is `nat`, because the type of 3 is `nat`, and thus the type does not have to be written explicitly. Using type variables in this way is called polymorphism and allows a single definition to be used for many different types with the same structure. For example, we can define lists of natural numbers, rational numbers, Booleans, etc. The notation `::` as an infix operator is used for `cons`. For example, `(cons 1 (cons 2 nil))` can be written as `(1::2::nil)`. Another notation for this list is `[1;2]` where elements are in brackets separated by a semi-colon. Using this notation, `(h::t)` represents a list with `h` as head and `t` as tail.

Using these definitions, we can write expressions with their types. For example, `X:nat` expresses that variable `X` is in the domain of natural numbers. The types used in our model include `nat`, `Q`, and `list` which denote natural numbers, rational numbers, and lists of elements respectively. These types and many useful properties about them can be found in Coq's standard libraries. There is also another type that comes in handy sometimes. This type is called `option` and like list, it is polymorphic and thus can be used at any other type. For example, we can have `option int`, `option Q`, or even `option (list nat)`. In general `option T`, where T is a type in Coq can have two types of values. It can be either `None` or `Some X`, where `X` has the type `T`. For instance, an `int option` can be `None` or `Some 5`. Option types can be employed to represent partial functions (We discuss functions in general in the next paragraph). We use the value `None` when the value does not exist and we use `Some` when we have the value. For example, consider the case where we need the last element of a list of natural numbers. If the list is empty, there is no such element, which we can represent as `None`, but if the list is not empty, we represent it as `(Some last)`, where `last` is the last element of the list and has the type `option int`. For instance, for the list `[]`, the value is `None` and for the list `[1;5;3]`, the value is `Some 3`. The inductive definition of option types is shown in Figure 5.

```
Inductive option (A: Type) : Type :=
  | None : option A
  | Some : A -> option A.
```

Figure 5. Inductive definition of options in Coq

Functions are a basic element of any functional programming language. The general form of a function in Coq is shown in Figure 6. `Definition` and `Fixpoint` are Coq keywords for defining non-recursive and recursive functions, respectively. A recursive function is a function that calls itself inside its body. Calling a function inside its body causes an error when `Definition` is used. After either one of these keywords comes the name that a programmer gives to the function.

```
Definition/Fixpoint <Function_Name>
  (<Input₁: Type of Input₁>) ... (<Inputₙ: Type of Inputₙ>) : <Output Type> :=
<Body of the function>.
```

Figure 6. General form for defining a function in Coq

Following the function name are the input arguments and their types. If two or more inputs have the same type, they can be grouped as, for example, `(X Y Z: Q)` which means all variables X, Y, and Z are rational numbers. Following the inputs is a colon, followed by the type of the output of the function. Finally, the body of the function is a Coq expression representing an expression to be evaluated, followed by a dot. To call a function, one should use the format <Function_Name> <Input₁> ...<Inputₙ>. For example, `(add x y)` is a function call to a function named `add` that takes x and y as its arguments.

A very useful function for lists, that we often use in our model, is appending two lists, which is called `app` in Coq. `app [1;3;4] [2;5;7;8]` returns `[1;3;4;2;5;7;8]`. ++ is infix notation that can be used for app. For example, `app l1 l2` can be written as `l1 ++ l2`.

Pattern matching is a useful method in Coq for case analysis. This feature is used, for instance, for distinguishing between base cases and recursive cases in recursive functions. Two samples of pattern matching are shown in Figure 7. The first pattern matching is for natural numbers. It has two separate cases for X. In the first one, it calculates something when X is 0. In the second one, it does another calculation when X is a successor of another natural number n and can be written as `S n`.

```
match X with
  | 0 => <Calculate something when X = 0>
  | S n => <Calculate something when X is successor of n>
end
match L with
  | [] => <Calculate something when L is an empty list>
  | h::t => <Calculate something when L has head h followed by tail t>
end
```

Figure 7. General form for pattern matching of natural numbers and lists in Coq

Coq can distinguish when a list is empty or not using pattern matching as shown in the second matching in Figure 7. L is either an empty list, written `[]` or has the form `h::t`. An example of a function from Coq's library that uses pattern matching is shown in Figure 8. If n is 0, m will be returned but if n is successor of p, the successor of the sum of p and m will be returned. + is the infix notation for this function. For example, `plus n m` can be written simply as `n + m`.

```
Fixpoint plus n m :=
  match n with
    | 0 => m
    | S p => S (plus p m)
  end.
```

Figure 8. Function `plus` for adding two natural numbers

In addition to the data types that are defined in Coq's libraries, new data types can be defined. One way to do so is defining records using the keyword `Record`. Records can have different fields with different types. For example, we can define a record that has three fields `Fieldnat`, `FieldQ`, and `ListField`, which have types natural number, rational number, and list of natural numbers, respectively. Figure 9 shows the Coq syntax for the definition of this record with one additional field called CR. Fields in Coq can represent conditions on other fields. For example, field CR in Figure 9 is a condition on the `Fieldnat` field stating that it must be greater than 7. After defining a record, it is a type like any other type, and so for example, we can have variables with the new record type. Variable S shown with the type `Sample_Record` in Figure 9 is an example. To refer to fields of variable S, we must write `(Fieldnat S)`, `(FieldQ S)`, `(ListField S)`. Records can be parameterized in Coq, which means they can accept input and define the record based on the given inputs. In Figure 9, `Sample_Record` is a record without any input. So, we can assume that it always defines the same record with same data and constraint fields which of course can have different values for different instances of the record.

```
Record Sample_Record := MakeSample {
   Fieldnat: nat;
   FieldQ: Q;
   ListField: list nat;
   CR: Fieldnat > 7
}.

S: Sample_Record
```

Figure 9. Definition of a record and a variable with the `Record` type in Coq

In Figure 10, a parameterized record is shown that accepts a list of natural numbers as an input called `Inputs`. This input can be used both to define data fields of the record `RecordwithInput` such as the field `ExtendedList`, which is the result of appending `ListField` to `Inputs` or to express a constraint field such as `Length_CR`, which guarantees that the number of elements in the `ListField` is greater than the number of elements in the `Inputs`.

To instantiate a variable of a parameterized record, we need to use @ followed by the name of the record and followed by the parameter value as shown in Figure 10 for the variable SP, which has the type `RecordwithInput`, which receives L as the input of type `list nat`. Parameterized records comes in handy for defining archetypes and composition of archetypes.

```
Record RecordwithInput {Inputs: list nat} := MakeRecordwithInput {
  Fieldnat: nat;
  FieldQ: Q;
  ListField: list nat;
  ExtendedList: ListField ++ Inputs;
  Length_CR: (length ListField) > (length Inputs)
}.


L: list nat
SP: (@RecordwithInput L)
```

Figure 10. Definition of a record that accepts input and a variable of the parameterized record in Coq

What makes Coq so powerful is its ability to help us prove properties, which we use to prove properties of our model. There are some methods for proving a theorem in mathematics such as induction, case analysis, proof by contradiction, etc. These methods are provided in Coq for proving theorems. There are several keywords for introducing theorems in Coq, including Theorem and Lemma. They are interpreted as equivalent keywords in Coq and having two different words for the same concept is just for the sake of readability. Figure 11 shows an example of a property of natural numbers. Recall that a theorem or lemma is a formula and hence it has the type Prop. In Figure 11, addsides is the name of the theorem and forall is a keyword in Coq for showing universal quantifier. We can start proving a theorem using the keyword Proof. The proof of addsides is shown following the Proof keyword. Commands, called *tactics* that are used in this proof will be explained later. Once a theorem is proved, it can be used as a lemma in proofs of lemmas and theorems appearing after it. Qed is the Coq keyword for marking the end of a proof.

```
Theorem addsides: forall a b c: nat,
        a = b -> a + c = b + c.
Proof.
        intros.
        rewrite H.
        reflexivity.
Qed.
```

Figure 11. Definition of a theorem in Coq

To prove a theorem, we need to use Coq tactics such as induction, destruct, rewrite, simpl, reflexivity, etc, some of which are described below. Figure 12 illustrates the notion of a proof state. It shows the proof of addsides just after the intros tactic in approved. Each hypothesis in a proof has the form H_Name :   H_Formula. For example, in Figure 12, H is the name of a hypothesis and it says that a = b. Also, variables and their types are shown. Here a, b, and c have type nat.

```
1 subgoal
a, b, c: nat  ⎫ Hypotheses
H: a = b      ⎭
________________________________
a + c = b + c    ◄── GOAL
```

Figure 12. An ongoing proof in Coq

intros. This tactic is for introducing information in the statement of a theorem or lemma such as universally quantified variables. For example, intros introduces a, b, and c as natural numbers which is why they appear above the line after applying intros in Figure 12. In addition, when there is an implication in the theorem, intros introduces its antecedent as a hypothesis. For example, H : a = b is introduced by intros in Figure 12.

simpl. This tactic can do a simplification on a goal or hypotheses by evaluating functions defined in Coq. For example, 0 + x = y is replaced by x = y after using the simpl tactic because 0 + x is evaluated to x using the definition of plus shown in Figure 8.

rewrite. This tactic is used for replacing a term with an equivalent one. For example, if we have a hypothesis H: a = b and the goal is to prove a + c = b + c, such as in the proof of the lemma in Figure 12, by asking Coq to apply rewrite H, the goal changes to b + c = b + c.

reflexivity. This tactic can be used to complete the proof of a goal when we end up with two equal terms such as b + c = b + c. In this case, using reflexivity finishes the proof. This tactic can only be applied on the goal and not hypotheses.

destruct. This tactic is a very useful for case analysis. We use this tactic usually when there is an inductive type appearing in the goal. For example, if we want to prove that l1 ++ (l2 ++ l3) = (l1 ++ l2) ++ l3, we can use destruct l1 as [| h t]. Recall that list has two constructors, which means that the proof is broken into two cases. In the notation [| h t], the vertical bar separates the two cases. The first case is for when l1 is nil. There is no information before the vertical bar because none is needed for this case. The second case needs two arguments. When `l1` is not an empty list, we need to tell Coq what its head is and what its tail is. Thus, `h` is the name of the head of `l1` and `t` is the name of the tail of `l1` in this case. These are arguments in the inductive case of the `list`. The first goal is `[] ++ (l2 ++ l3) = ([] ++ l2) ++ l3` because in the first case Coq considers `l1` an empty list. The second goal is `h::t ++ (l2 ++ l3) = (h::t ++ l2) ++ l3` because in this case `l1=h::t`. Both subgoals have to be proved to complete the proof.

induction. This tactic applies induction, a powerful proof method in Coq as well as in mathematics. Similar to `destruct`, we use this tactic when a term in the hypothesis list has a type that is inductively defined. An induction hypothesis is added for all inductive cases. Considering the same example above, if we want to prove that `l1 ++ (l2 ++ l3) = (l1 ++ l2) ++ l3`, we can use `induction l1 as [ | h t IH]`. `[ | h t IH]` has the same meaning as above for `destruct` except `IH` which is the name of the induction hypothesis. Using `induction` creates two subgoals like `destruct` which are exactly the same subgoals as in that case. The only difference is that this time we have the induction hypothesis `IH` added to our hypotheses which is `t ++ (l2 ++ l3) = (t ++ l2) ++ l3`. This new hypothesis assumes that our goal is true for the tail of the list. This induction hypothesis is very useful for proving the goal. Again, both subgoals have to be proved to complete the proof.

inversion. This tactic has many applications including proof by contradiction and breaking a hypothesis into its inductive cases. If there is a contradiction in one of the hypotheses, the proof of the goal can be completed by using `inversion` on that hypothesis. Mostly, contradictions come from equality of two inductive cases in a definition. For example, if `H: h::t = []` is a hypothesis in a proof, by using `inversion H`, the proof will be completed. Two inductive cases cannot be equal and this is a contradiction. For example, an empty list cannot be equal to a non-empty list with a head and a tail. Also, another helpful application of `inversion` is decomposing a hypothesis. For example if there is a hypothesis `H: a = b /\ c = d` (where `/\` represents logical conjunction in Coq, to be explained later), we can use `inversion H as [H1 H2]` to get `H1: a = b` and `H2: c = d`. `H1` and `H2` are the names the user wants to give to the new hypotheses in `H`. `inversion` is a powerful tactic whose full behavior is not explained here.

In addition, we use many other tactics that we do not explain here.

3.1 Propositions and Booleans

As mentioned earlier, `Prop` is the type of formulas in Coq. Coq also has Booleans, called `bool`. The main difference is `bool` is a data type, hence it is an element of the type `Set`. `bool` is defined inductively in Coq as shown in Figure 13.

```
Inductive bool : Set :=
  | true : bool
  | false: bool.
```

Figure 13. Inductive definition of `bool` in Coq

There is no recursive case in the definition of `bool` because it is a simple type with two possible values. Note that `True` and `False` with capitalized first letter have the type `Prop` but `true` and `false` with lowercase first letter have the type `bool`. `bool` is an inductive datatype like natural numbers and it can be used in defining functions on Coq data. Functions `andb`, `orb`, and `negb` are all defined in Figure 14.

```
Definition andb (a b: bool): bool :=
  match a with
    | false => false
    | true => b
  end.

Definition orb (a b: bool): bool :=
  match a with
    | false => b
    | true => true
  end.

Definition negb (a: bool): bool :=
  match a with
    | false => true
    | true => false
  end.
```

Figure 14. Definition of Boolean and, or, and negation in Coq

In addition, Coq has an if expression of the form `if <X> then <Y> else <Z>` where `<X>` must be `bool`. In this instruction, `<X>` can only be replaced by a Boolean value, which has the type `bool`. To illustrate the difference further, assume `X` is a `bool` and we want to prove that when a = b, then X is true. We cannot write this formula as a = b -> X, because Coq accepts only a formula as the consequence of an implication. So, the formula should be a = b -> X = true. X = true is an equality comparison and it has the type Prop. In Coq, the connectives for conjunction, disjunction, and negation are written /\ (as mentioned), \/, and ~. Thus, if A and B are formulas in Prop, so are A /\ B, A \/ B, and ~A.

3.2 Useful functions for our Neural Network Model

In this section, we introduce some functions that we use for our model in the next chapter. The first function is beq_nat, which is a short for Boolean equality of natural numbers. This function is shown in Figure 15. It takes two natural numbers as input and returns true if they are equal and false otherwise. In Figure 15, there is multiple pattern matching. Each natural number has two inductive cases, and thus, there are four possible cases. If both of them are 0, they are equal, so beq_nat returns true for the first case. If one of them is 0 and the other one is a successor of another natural number, obviously they cannot be equal. The second and third cases of beq_nat cover this inequality. The last case of beq_nat applies when both inputs are successors of another natural number. In this case, equality of those numbers is checked by a recursive call. Thus, a = b is a formula in Coq (an expression of type Prop) and (beq_nat a b) is an expression of type bool which may be simplified by evaluating the beq_nat function.

```
Fixpoint beq_nat (n m: nat) : bool :=
  match n, m with
    | O, O => true
    | O, S q => false
    | S p, O => false
    | S p, S q => beq_nat p q
  end.
```

Figure 15. Definition of Boolean equality of natural numbers in Coq

As mentioned earlier, Q is the type for rational numbers. We do not go into detail of how rational numbers are defined in the Coq library because it is not necessary to define our model, but we need to discuss three useful functions for comparing rational numbers. The first function called Qle_bool is defined in the Coq library. This function takes two rational numbers and returns true if the first one is less than or equal to the second one. Operator <= of type Prop is also defined in the library of rational numbers. If a and b have type Q, then a <= b is an element of Prop, while `Qle_bool a b` is a bool. `Qlt_bool` is another function that it is used in our code. We define it since it was not already available in the Coq library. Its definition is shown in Figure 16. It takes two rational numbers and returns `true` if the first one is less than the second one and `false` otherwise.

```
Definition Qlt_bool (a b: Q): bool :=
    andb (Qle_bool a b)(negb (Qeq_bool a b)).
```

Figure 16. Definition of `Qlt_bool` for comparing rational numbers in Coq

This function uses `Qle_bool` and another function for rational numbers called `Qeq_bool`. `Qeq_bool` is defined in Coq library for checking equality of two rational numbers. It returns `true` when its arguments are equal and `false` otherwise. There is also equality on rational numbers. In summary, <=, <, and = are defined for Prop, while `Qle_bool`, `Qlt_bool`, and `Qeq_bool` are Boolean operators.

3.3 Useful List Functions for Archetypes and Their Coupling

Another function that we use from the Coq library, particularly for proving properties about archetypes and their composition, is `List.nth`, which takes three arguments. The first argument is the index n, the second one is the list L and the third one is a default value d. The function returns the nth element of L if there is such an element and d if the number of elements in L is less than n. This function is shown in Figure 17. T can be replaced by any type in Figure 17.

```
Fixpoint List.nth (n: nat) (L:list T) (d: T): T :=
    match L with
    | [] => d
    | h::t => if (beq_nat n 0) then h
                else List.nth (n - 1) t d
    end.
```

Figure 17. Definition of `List.nth` for extracting the nth element of a list in Coq

Two of most commonly used list functions are hd and tl which return the head and the tail of a given list respectively. hd takes two arguments which are a default value and the list but tl takes only the list. hd returns the default value if the list is empty but tl returns an empty list when the list is empty and it does not need an extra argument for that. These functions are shown in Figure 18. Once again T can be replaced by any type in Figure 18.

```
Definition hd (d: nat) (L: list T): T :=
  match L with
    | [] => d
    | h::t => h
  end.
Definition tl (L: list T): list T :=
  match L with
    | [] => []
    | h::t => t
  end.
```

Figure 18. Definition of hd and tl for finding the head and the tail of a list in Coq

Another useful function in the list library is called skipn. This function takes a natural number n and a list and returns a list which contains all elements of the given list after skipping its first n elements. For example, skipn 2 [10; 2; 6; 8; 5] is [6; 8; 5]. When n is 0, the answer is the list itself and when n is greater than the number of elements in the list, skipn returns an empty list. This function is shown in Figure 19. T is any valid type in Coq in Figure 19.

```
Fixpoint skipn (n: nat) (L: list T): list T :=
  match n with
    | O => L
    | S m => match L with
               | [] => []
               | h::t => skipn m t
             end
  end.
```

Figure 19. Definition of skipn for finding the list by omitting the first n elements of a list in Coq

Chapter 4

Modelling Leaky Integrate and Fire Model Neurons in Coq

We illustrate our encoding of neural networks in Coq by beginning with the code in Figure 20. We use Coq's record structure to define a neuron. This record includes five fields with their types, and four fields, which represent constraints that the first five fields must satisfy according to the LI&F model mentioned in Chapter 2. The types include natural numbers, rational numbers, and lists.

```
Record Neuron := MakeNeuron {
  Output: list nat;
  Weights: list Q;
  Leak_Factor: Q;
  Tau: Q;
  Current: Q;
  Output_Bin: Bin_List Output;
  Leak_Range: Qle_bool 0 Leak_Factor = true /\ Qle_bool Leak_Factor 1 = true;
  PosTau: Qlt_bool 0 Tau = true;
  WRange: WeightInRange Weights = true
}.
```

Figure 20. Coq code defining a neuron and the weighted sum of its inputs

In particular, a neuron's output (`Output`) is represented as a list of natural numbers, with one entry for each time step. The weights attached to the inputs of the neuron (`Weights`) are stored in a list of rational numbers, one for each input in some designated order. The leak factor (`Leak_Factor`), the firing threshold (`Tau`), and the most recent neuron membrane potential (`Current`) are rational numbers. With respect to the four conditions, the definition of `Bin_List` is shown in Figure 21. `Bin_List` takes a list of natural numbers and returns `True` if the list contains only 0s and 1s.

```
Fixpoint Bin_List (In: list nat) : Prop :=
match In with
  | nil => True
  | h::t => (orb (beq_nat h 0%nat) (beq_nat h 1%nat)) = true /\ (Bin_List t)
end.
```

Figure 21. Definition of `Bin_List` function for checking that a list is a binary list

Note that Bin_List is a predicate. The output type of Bin_List is a Prop. Recall that Prop is a basic Coq data type, which represents any formula in Coq and beq_nat is a function defined in Coq to check if two natural numbers are equal and it returns a Boolean. The default type of 0 and 1 is rational number. In our code, when we write a specific number, if the type is not Q, then we must annotate the number with its type. The arguments of beq_nat must be natural numbers, which is why 0%nat and 1%nat are used instead of 0 and 1. (orb (beq_nat h 0%nat) (beq_nat h 1%nat)) = true is a formula, which means it has the type Prop. The constraint Bin_List Output in the definition of Neuron ensures that output list of neurons always contains only 0s and 1s.

The second constraint makes sure that Leak_Factor is between 0 and 1 inclusive using Qle_bool.The third constraint, which is called PosTau, expresses that Tau must be positive using Qlt_bool. These constraints are all required by the LI&F model. The definition of WeightInRange, used in the fourth constraint, is shown in Figure 22. WeightInRange takes as input a list of weights of a neuron and checks that all of them are between -1 and 1. Recursion is used to check every member of the input list one by one.

```
Fixpoint WeightInRange (Weights: list Q) : bool :=
  match Weights with
  | nil => true
  | h::t => andb (Qle_bool h 1) (Qle_bool (-(1)) h)
  end.
```

Figure 22. Definition of WeightInRange function for checking weights range of neurons

Given a neuron N, recall that (Output N) denotes its first field, and similarly for the others. To create a new neuron with values O, W, L, T, and C of the appropriate types, and proofs P1,..., P4 of the four constraints, we write (MakeNeuron O W L T C P1 P2 P3 P4).

In Figure 23, the definition of potential function is shown, which implements the weighted sum of the inputs of a neuron, which is an important part of the calculation in Equation (1) in Definition 1. In this recursive function, there are two arguments: Weights of the form $[w_1; \ldots; w_m]$ and Inputs of the form $[x_1; \ldots; x_m]$. The function returns an element of type Q. Its definition uses pattern matching on both inputs simultaneously.

```
Fixpoint potential (Weights: list Q) (Inputs: list nat): Q :=
  match Weights, Inputs with
    | nil, nil => 0
    | nil, _  => 0
    | _, nil => 0
    | h1::t1, h2::t2 => if (beq_nat h2 0%nat)
                        then (potential t1 t2)
                        else (potential t1 t2) + h1
  end.
```

Figure 23. Definition of a function for `Weights` and `Inputs` element by element product in Equation (1)

Although, we always call the potential function with two lists of equal length, Coq requires functions to be total; when two lists do not have equal length, we return a "default" value of 0. Also, when we call this function, `Inputs`, which is the second argument of the function, is always a binary list (containing only the natural numbers 0 and 1). Thus, when the head of this list h2 is 0, we do not need to add anything to the final sum because anything multiplied by 0 is 0. In this case, we just call the function recursively on the remaining weights and inputs t1 and t2. On the other hand, when h2 is 1, we need to add h1, the head of `Weights` to the final sum, which again is the recursive call on t1 and t2.

Figure 24 shows the `NextPotential` function, which implements $p(t)$ from Equation (1). Recall that `(Current N)` is the most recent potential value of the neuron, which is $p(t-1)$ in Equation (1). `(Qle_bool (Tau N) (Current N))` represents $\tau \leq p(t-1)$ and we use the function defined in Figure 23 for the part calculating the weighted sum of the neuron inputs. Finally, `(Leak_Factor N) * (Current N)` implements $r \cdot p(t-1)$.

```
Definition NextPotential (N: Neuron) (Inputs: list nat): Q :=
  if (Qle_bool (Tau N) (Current N)
  then (potential (Weights N) Inputs)
  else (potential (Weights N) Inputs) + (Leak_Factor N) * (Current N).
```

Figure 24. Definition of the potential function for calculating Equation (1) in Coq

Figure 25 shows the definition of function `NextOutput`. This function calculates the next output of the neuron which is $y(t)$ in Equation (2) of Definition 1. Recall that `(NextPotential N Inputs)` shown in Figure 24 calculates $p(t)$. Thus, the expression `(Qle_bool (Tau N) (NextPotential N Inputs))` expresses the condition $\tau \leq p(t)$.

```
Definition NextOuput (N: Neuron) (Inputs: list nat): nat :=
  if (Qle_bool (Tau N) (NextPotential N Inputs))
  then 1%nat
  else 0%nat.
```

Figure 25. `NextOutput` function for calculation the next output of a neuron

In our model, the state of a neuron is represented by the `Output` and `Current` fields. The
`Output` field of a neuron in the initial state is `[0%nat]`, which denotes a list of length 1
containing only 0. The Current field represents the initial potential, which is set to 0. A neuron
changes state by processing input. After processing a list of n inputs, the `Output` field is a list of
length n + 1 containing 0's and 1's, and the `Current` field is set to the value of the potential
after processing these n inputs. State change occurs by applying the `NextNeuron` function in
Figure 26 to a neuron and a list of inputs.

```
Definition NextNeuron (N: Neuron) (Inputs: list nat): Neuron:= MakeNeuron
  ((NextOutput N Inputs)::(Output N))
  (Weights N)
  (Leak_Factor N)
  (Tau N)
  (NextPotential N Inputs)
  (NextOutput_Bin_List N Inputs (Output_Bin N))
  (Leak_Range N)
  (PosTau N)
  (WRange N) .
```

Figure 26. `NextNeuron` function for returning a neuron in its next state after applying an input

As is typical in functional programming, we represent a neuron at its later state by creating a new
record with the new values for `Output` and `Current` and other values directly copied over. We
store the values in the `Output` field in reverse order, which simplifies proofs by induction over
lists, which we use regularly in our Coq proofs. Thus, the most recent output of the neuron is at
the head of the list. We can see this in the code in Figure 26, where the new value of the output is
`((NextOutput N Inputs)::(Output N))`. The next output of the neuron is at the head,
followed by the previous outputs. `(NextPotential N Inputs)` is the new value for
`(Current N)`. Recall that `(Current N)` is the most recent value of potential value of the
neuron or $p(t-1)$. So, for calculating the next potential value of the neuron or $p(t)$, the
`NextPotential` function in Figure 24 is called.

Following the new values for each field of the neuron, we have proofs of the four constraints. The first requires a lemma `NextOutput_Bin_List`, whose statement and proof are shown in Figure 27, which allows us to prove that the new longer list is still a binary list. Proofs of the other three constraints are carried over exactly from the original neuron, since they are about components of the neuron that do not change.

```
Lemma NextOutput_Bin_List: forall (N: Neuron) (Inputs: list nat),
      Bin_List (Output N) -> Bin_List (NextOutput N Inputs::Output N).
Proof.
      intros. simpl. split.
    - unfold NextOutput.
      destruct (Qle_bool (Tau N) (NextPotential N Inputs))
      + simpl. reflexivity.
      + simpl. reflexivity.
    - apply H.
Qed.
```

Figure 27. `NextOutput_Bin_List` proof to show the output list of a neuron remains
a binary list after adding the new output

The `NextOutput_Bin_List` lemma states that if the output of a neuron is a binary list, then applying the next input list to its inputs, it will stay a binary list. `NextOutput N Inputs` is the new head of neuron `N`'s output list in the definition of `NextOutput_Bin_List`. In the proof of this theorem, some common tactics of Coq, described in Chapter 3, are used such as `destruct`, `simpl`, and `reflexivity`.

```
Definition ResetNeuron (N: Neuron): Neuron:= MakeNeuron
    ([0%nat])
    (Weights N)
    (Leak_Factor N)
    (Tau N)
    (0)
    (Reset_Output)
    (Leak_Range N)
    (PosTau N)
    (WRange N).
```

Figure 28. Definition of `ResetNeuron` function for resetting a neuron

To reinitialize a neuron to the initial state as described above, the `ResetNeuron` function is used. This function takes any `Neuron` as input, and returns a new one, with the `Output`, `Current`, and `Output_Bin` fields reset to `[0%nat]`, `0`, and `Reset_Output` respectively while keeping the others. `ResetNeuron` is shown in Figure 28. `Reset_Output` is just a simple lemma that states that `[0%nat]` is a binary list.

Chapter 5

Properties of Neurons and Their Proofs

As mentioned earlier, we prove five basic properties of the LI&F model of neurons in this chapter. All of them have been fully verified in Coq. Sections 5.1 to 5.5 present the properties and their mathematical proofs. Section 5.6 discusses their implementation and verification in Coq in more detail. The reason that both mathematical proofs and verifications are important is that mathematical proofs contain human mistakes. Particularly, they can suffer from incorrect assumptions. Verifications of these proofs make sure that the proof is reliable and assumptions are correctly made to lead the proof to its conclusion.

In this chapter, we give a more mathematical account when stating properties and presenting their proofs. We use some conventions to enhance readability and omit some details that are specific to the way we implement them in Coq. In all of the statements of the properties, we omit the assumption that the input sequence of the neuron is a binary list and contains only 0s and 1s. It is of course, included in the Coq code. We state our properties using pretty-printed Coq syntax, with some abbreviations for our own definitions. For instance, we use mathematical fonts and conventions for Coq text, e.g., (Output N) is written $Output(N)$, (Tau N) is written $\tau(N)$, (Weights N) is written $w(N)$, (Leak_Factor N) is written $r(N)$, and (Current N) is written $p(N)$. In addition, if $w(N)$ is a list of the form $[w_1; ...; w_n]$ for some $n \geq 0$, for $i = 1, ..., n$, we often write $w_i(N)$ to denote w_i. Function length is used in Coq for getting number of elements in a list. In other words, (length nlist) represents the length of the list nlist. We will write it as $length(nlist)$ in our mathematical proofs. Also, we use + instead of ++ to show list concatenation. Recall that operator ++ is for appending two lists in Coq. In addition, although for a neuron N, the list $Output(N)$ is encoded in reverse order in our Coq model, when presenting properties and their proofs here, we use forward order.

5.1 The Delayer Effect for a Single-Input Neuron

We start with a property about a simple neuron, which has only one input. We refer to this neuron as a *single-input neuron*. The first property is called the *delayer effect* property. Recall that a neuron is in an inactive state when it is initialized using the `ResetNeuron` function shown in Figure 28, which means the output of a neuron at time 0 is 0. When a neuron has only one input, and the weight of that input is greater than or equal to its activation threshold, then the neuron transfers the input sequence to the output without any change (except for a "delay" of length 1). For instance, if a single input neuron receives 0100110101 as its input sequence, it will produce 00100110101 as output. Neurons that have this property are not functional neurons. They are mainly just transferring signals. Humans have some of this type of neurons in their auditory system. This property is expressed as Property 1.

Property 1. $\forall$ $(N: neuron)$ $(input: list\ nat)$,

$$Bin\_List(input) \wedge length\big(w(N)\big) = 1 \wedge w_1(N) \geq \tau(N) \rightarrow Output(N') = [0] + input$$

In the above statement, N' denotes the neuron obtained by initializing N and then processing the input (using `ResetNeuron` in Figure 28 and repeated applications of `NextNeuron` in Figure 26). We use this convention in stating all of our properties. $Bin\_List(input)$ states that $input$ is a binary list, which means it contains only 0s and 1s. Recall that we have the predicate `Bin_List`, which is shown in Figure 21 that is equivalent to `True` when a list of natural numbers is a binary list in Coq. Note that in Definition 1, Equation (1), p is a function of time. Time in our Coq model is encoded as the position in the output list. If $Output(N)$ has length t, then $p(N)$ stores $p(t - 1)$ from Equation (1). If we then apply `NextNeuron` to N and the next input obtaining N', then $Output(N')$ has length $t + 1$ and $p(N')$ stores the value $p(t)$ from Equation (1).

In order to prove Property 1, we need the following lemma, which states that when a neuron has one input and its input weight is greater than or equal to its threshold, the potential value of that neuron is always non-negative.

Lemma 1. $\forall$ $(N: neuron)$ $(input: list\ nat)$,

$$Bin\_List(input) \wedge length\big(w(N)\big) = 1 \wedge w_1(N) \geq \tau(N) \rightarrow p(N') \geq 0$$

As explained above $p(N')$ is the most recent value of the potential function of neuron N, i.e., the one obtained after processing all of the input values.

Proof *(of Lemma 1)*. The proof is by induction on the length of the input sequence.

Base case: $input = []$ (the empty list). If there is no input in the input sequence, the neuron will keep its initial status, i.e., $N = N'$. So, $p(N') = 0$. Therefore, $p(N') \geq 0$.

Induction case: we assume that the property is true for $input$ and we must show that it holds for some $input'$ of the form $(input + [h])$ for some additional input value h. Let N' be the neuron resulting from processing $input$, and let N'' be the input after processing $input'$. By the induction hypothesis, we know $p(N') \geq 0$ and we must prove that $p(N'') \geq 0$.

Note that $\tau(N) = \tau(N') = \tau(N'')$ and $w_1(N) = w_1(N') = w_1(N'')$, so we use them interchangeably. We break this proof into two cases depending on whether or not $p(N') \geq \tau(N')$.

First, let us assume that $p(N') \geq \tau(N')$. $Bin\_List(input)$ implies that the input sequence contains only 0s and 1s, we know that $h = 0$ or $h = 1$. We calculate $p(N'')$, which as stated, corresponds to $p(t)$ in Equation (1), i.e., the potential value of the neuron at time t; the value $p(N')$ represents $p(t - 1)$ in this definition. Because of our assumption, only the first clause of Equation (1) applies, with two possibilities depending on the value of h:

$$p(N'') = w_1(N') \cdot 0 = 0 \text{ or}$$

$$p(N'') = w_1(N') \cdot 1 = w_1(N').$$

In the first case, $p(N'') = 0 \geq 0$. In the second case, $p(N'') = w_1(N')$ and we know $w_1(N') \geq \tau(N)$ by assumption, and $\tau(N) > 0$ because, by definition, the activation threshold of any neuron is a positive value.

Second, we assume that $p(N') < \tau(N)$. So, again because the input contains only 0s and 1s, we know that $h = 0$ or $h = 1$. By the second clause of the definition of p in Equation (1), we have:

$$p(N'') = w_1(N') \cdot 0 + r(N') \cdot p(N') = r(N') \cdot p(N') \text{ or}$$

$$p(N'') = w_1(N') \cdot 1 + r(N') \cdot p(N') = w_1(N') + r(N') \cdot p(N').$$

In the first case, $r(N')$ is non-negative by definition and $p(N')$ is non-negative by the induction hypothesis. Thus, $r(N') \cdot p(N') \geq 0$. For the second case, we also have that $w_1(N') \geq \tau(N') > 0$, and thus the sum of two non-negative numbers is also non-negative.

This completes the proof, thus showing that it is always the case that the value of the potential of a single input neuron with an input weight greater than or equal to its activation threshold, is non-negative.

We use Lemma 1 here to prove Property 1.

Proof *(of Property 1)*. The proof is by induction on the length of the input sequence as follows.

Base case: $input = []$ (the empty list). If there is no input in the input sequence, the neuron will keep its initial status, i.e., $N = N'$. So, $Output(N') = [0]$. Therefore, $Output(N') = [0] = [0] + [] = [0] + input$.

Induction case: We assume that the property is true for $input$ and we must show that it holds for some $input'$ of the form $(input + [h])$ for some additional input value h. Let N' be the neuron resulting from processing $input$, and let N'' be the neuron after processing $input'$. By the induction hypothesis, we know $Output(N') = [0] + input$ and we must prove that $Output(N'') = [0] + input'$.

Note that $\tau(N) = \tau(N') = \tau(N'')$ and similar equalities hold for r and w_1, so we use them interchangeably. Because $input$ is a binary list, we know that $h = 0$ or $h = 1$. We break this into two different cases, depending on the value of h.

First, we assume that $input' = input + [0]$ and we prove that $Output(N'') = Output(N') + [0]$. In this case, the most recent input to the neuron is 0. Again, to relate this to Equation (1), let t be the time at which we process the last input. We calculate $p(N'')$, which corresponds to $p(t)$, i.e., the potential value of the neuron at time t; also, the value $p(N')$ represents $p(t-1)$ in this definition. Using the first and second clauses of Equation (1), respectively, the value is one of:

$$p(N'') = w_1(N') \cdot 0 = 0 \text{ or } p(N'') = w_1(N') \cdot 0 + r(N') \cdot p(N').$$

In the first case, $p(N'') = 0$ and we know $0 < \tau(N)$, because $\tau(N)$ is always positive. So, by the second clause of Equation (2) in Definition 1, the next output of the neuron is 0. The other case, which comes from the second clause of Equation (1) has the same result. In this case, the condition on this clause says that $p(N') < \tau(N')$ and we must show that $p(N'') = r(N') \cdot p(N') < \tau(N)$. Recall that $r(N')$, the leak factor of the neuron, is between 0 and 1. So, multiplying any number that is less than a positive number by a value between 0 and 1 gives a value that is smaller than or equal to the original number. Therefore, by Equation (2), the next output of the neuron is 0 again. We can conclude now that by adding 0 to the input sequence, a 0 is produced in the output. Thus, $Output(N'') = Output(N') + [0]$. Using our induction hypothesis, we have:

$$Output(N'') = Output(N') + [0] = [0] + input + [0] = 0 + input'.$$

Second, we assume that $input' = input + [1]$ and we prove that $Output(N'') = Output(N') + [1]$. In this case, the most recent input of the neuron is 1. Again, we calculate the potential value of N'' using Equation (1):

$$p(N'') = w_1(N') \cdot 1 = w_1(N') \text{ or}$$

$$p(N'') = w_1(N') \cdot 1 + r(N') \cdot p(N') = w_1(N') + r(N') \cdot p(N').$$

In the first case, when $p(N'') = w_1(N')$, we know that $w_1(N) \geq \tau(N)$ by assumption in the statement of the property, we know that $w_1(N) = w_1(N')$ as discussed, and thus $p(N'') \geq \tau(N)$. So, by Equation (2), the next output of the neuron is 1. In the second case, $p(N') \geq 0$ according to Lemma 1, and it is always the case that $r(N') \geq 0$, so we can conclude that $r(N') \cdot p(N') \geq 0$. Because $w_1(N) \geq \tau(N)$ and adding a non-negative value to the greater side of an inequality keeps it that way, we can conclude that $p(N'') = w_1(N') + r(N') \cdot p(N') \geq \tau(N)$. Therefore, again by Equation (2), the next output of the neuron is 1 again. Thus, we can conclude in both cases that by adding 1 to the input sequence, a 1 is produced in the output. Thus, $Output(N'') = Output(N') + [1]$. Using our induction hypothesis, we have:

$$Output(N'') = Output(N') + [1] = [0] + input + [1] = 0 + input'.$$

This completes the proof.

5.2 The Filter Effect for a Single-Input Neuron

The next property we consider is also about single-input neurons. When a neuron has only one input, and the weight of that input is less than its activation threshold, the neuron passes on the value 1 once as output for each sequence of n consecutive 1s in the input. All 1s in the input are replaced by 0 except for the n-th one, the $2n$-th one, the $3n$-th one, etc. The other 1s are filtered out. For instance, let $n = 3$. Then if a single input neuron with this effect receives 01110010111 as input, it will produce 000010000001 as the output sequence, where a 1 appears after having seen three 1s in the input (the output sequence is one longer than the input because of the leading 0). As a consequence, there are never two consecutive 1s in the output sequence. This consequence is called the *filter effect*. Most neurons in the human neural network have the filter effect because their input weight is less than their activation threshold. Normally, more than one input is needed to activate a human neuron. In biology, this property is often called the *integrator effect*.

Property 2. $\forall\,(N: neuron)\,(input: list\,nat),$

$$Bin\_List(input) \wedge length\big(w(N)\big) = 1 \wedge w_1(N) < \tau(N) \rightarrow 11 \notin Output(N')$$

Note that in the statement above, $11 \notin Output(N')$ means there are no two consecutive 1s in the list $Output(N')$.

Proof *(of Property 2).* We prove this theorem again by induction on the structure of the input list.

Base case: $input = []$. If there is no input in the input sequence, the neuron will keep its initial status, i.e., $N = N'$. So, $Output(N') = [0]$. Therefore, $11 \notin Output(N') = [0]$.

Induction case: we assume that the property is true for *input* and we must show that it holds for some *input'* of the form $(input + [h])$ for some additional input value h. Let N' be the neuron resulting from processing *input*, and let N'' be the input after processing *input'*. By the induction hypothesis, we know $11 \notin Output(N')$ and we must prove that $11 \notin Output(N'')$.

Because we know that a neuron produces only 0 and 1 as output values, we know that $Output(N'') = Output(N') + [0]$ or $Output(N'') = Output(N') + [1]$. For the first case, we are done, because when 11 does not appear in a sequence, then by adding a 0 to the end of that sequence, there is still no 11 in that sequence.

The second case here is a bit more complicated. We need to split this case into two subcases. First, let us assume that the last produced output in $Output(N')$ is 0, i.e., $Output(N')$ has the form $Seq + [0]$. So, it is clear that by adding a 1 to a sequence, which ended with 0 and does not have any 11, the resulting sequence does not have any 11 as a substring. Thus, we can conclude that $11 \notin Output(N') \rightarrow 11 \notin Seq + [0] \rightarrow 11 \notin Seq + [0] + [1] \rightarrow 11 \notin Output(N') + [1] \rightarrow 11 \notin Output(N'')$.

Now for the second subcase, let us assume that the last produced output in $Output(N')$ is 1, i.e., $Output(N')$ has the form $Seq + [1]$. In this case, we have to prove that the next output is 0. Because the last produced output in $Output(N')$ is 1, we know that $p(N') \geq \tau(N')$. So, $p(N'') = h \cdot w_1(N')$ and because $Bin\_List(input)$ implies that $h = 0$ or $h = 1$, we can conclude that $p(N'') = w_1(N')$ or $p(N'') = 0$. In the first case, according to the property assumption, we know that $w_1(N) < \tau(N)$, and thus $p(N'') = w_1(N') = w_1(N) < \tau(N)$, and in the second case, because $\tau(N)$ is a positive value we have $p(N'') = 0 < \tau(N)$. Thus, by Equation (2), the next produced output is 0. Therefore, $11 \notin Output(N') \rightarrow 11 \notin Seq + [1] \rightarrow 11 \notin Seq + [1] + [0] \rightarrow 11 \notin Output(N') + [1] \rightarrow 11 \notin Output(N'')$.

This completes the proof.

We state a simple property here, which is a direct corollary of Property 1 and Property 2. This property, which states that a LI&F neuron can show either the delayer effect or the filter effect, is expressed as follows:

Property 3. $\forall\ (N\colon neuron)\ (input\colon list\ nat),$

$Bin\_List(input) \wedge length\big(w(N)\big) \rightarrow Output(N') = [0] + input \vee 11 \notin Output(N')$

Proof *(of Property 3)*. The proof of this property is straightforward. We consider two cases for this proof. We know that either $w_1(N) \geq \tau(N)$ or $w_1(N) < \tau(N)$. If $w_1(N) \geq \tau(N)$, we have all of the assumptions of Property 1 and we can conclude that $Output(N') = [0] + input$. In other words, $Bin\_List(input) \wedge length\big(w(N)\big) \wedge w_1(N) \geq \tau(N) \rightarrow Output(N') = [0] + input$. On the other hand, if $w_1(N) < \tau(N)$, we have all of the assumptions of Property 2 and we can conclude that $11 \notin Output(N')$. In other words, $Bin\_List(input) \wedge length\big(w(N)\big) \wedge w_1(N) < \tau(N) \rightarrow 11 \notin Output(N')$.

This completes the proof.

5.3 The Inhibitor Effect for a Single Input-Neuron

The next property is an important one because it has the potential to help us detect inactive zones of the brain. Normally, a human neuron does not have negative weights for all of its inputs but when one or more positive weight inputs are out of order because of some kind of disability, this property can occur. It is called the *inhibitor effect* because it is important for proving properties of the archetype in Figure 2(e). We consider here the single neuron case. When a neuron has only one input and the weight of that input is less than 0, then the neuron is inactive, which means that for any input, the neuron cannot emit 1 as output. i.e., if a signal reaches this neuron, it will not pass through. As with the other properties, the input sequence has an arbitrary finite length. This property is expressed as follows.

Property 4. $\forall\ (N\colon neuron)\ (input\colon list\ nat),$

$Bin\_List(input) \wedge length\big(w(N)\big) = 1 \wedge w_1(N) < 0 \rightarrow 1 \notin Output(N')$

Similar to Property 2, in the statement above, $1 \notin Output(N')$ means there is no 1 in the list $Output(N')$.

Proof *(of Property 4).* We prove this property using induction on the input length again.

Base case: $input = [\,]$. If there is no input in the input sequence, the neuron will keep its initial status, i.e., $N = N'$. So, $Output(N') = [0]$. Therefore, $1 \notin Output(N') = [0]$.

Induction case: we assume that the property is true for $input$ and we must show that it holds for some $input'$ of the form $(input + [h])$ for some additional input value h. Let N' be the neuron resulting from processing $input$, and let N'' be the input after processing $input'$. By the induction hypothesis, we know $1 \notin Output(N')$ and we must prove that $1 \notin Output(N'')$.

Let t be the time at which we produced the most recent output. So, $p(N'')$ corresponds to $p(t)$ and $p(N')$ corresponds to $p(t-1)$. Again, note that $\tau(N) = \tau(N') = \tau(N'')$ and similar equalities hold for r and w_1, so we use them interchangeably. Using the induction hypothesis, we know that $1 \notin Output(N')$. So, the last produced output in $Output(N')$ is 0. Thus, $p(N') = p(t-1) < \tau(N')$. That makes $p(t) = p(N'') = w_1(N'') \cdot h + r(N'') \cdot p(N')$. We need to consider two cases, which are $h = 0$ and $h = 1$.

In the first case, $p(N'') = r(N'') \cdot p(N')$. We can conclude that $p(N'') = r(N'') \cdot p(N') < \tau(N')$ because $p(N') < \tau(N')$ by the property assumption and it is multiplied by $r(N')$, the leak factor, which is between 0 and 1. Recall that $\tau(N')$ is a positive value. Thus, the next output is 0 in this case and $1 \notin Output(N') + [0] = Output(N'')$.

In the second case, $p(N'') = w_1(N'') + r(N'') \cdot p(N')$. With the same reasoning as the previous case, we can say that $r(N'') \cdot p(N') < \tau(N')$. Because $w_1(N')$ is a negative value, adding it to the left side of the inequality makes it smaller and the inequality still holds. Thus, $p(N'') = w_1(N'') + r(N'') \cdot p(N') < \tau(N')$. Therefore, the next output is 0 in this case too and $1 \notin Output(N') + [0] = Output(N'')$.

This completes the proof.

The inhibitor effect expressed in Property 4 has a more general version, which states the same result for a neuron with more than one input. For a neuron with multiple inputs, when all input weights are less than or equal to 0, then the neuron is inactive and cannot pass any signal. In other words, this neuron cannot produce 1 in its output. Although, there is no neuron whose input weights are all non-positive in the human neural network, this property can lead to a form of disability. If a neuron has both positive and non-positive input weights but inputs with positive weights are inactive, which means they either do not receive 1 as input or they do not pass the signal to the neuron, that neuron is inactive and cannot fire spikes. Inactive neurons can create a chain of disabled neurons. For instance, assume that neuron N1 is inactive and the only positive input of neuron N2 comes from the output of neuron N1. Knowing that N1 is inactive and cannot produce 1 in its output, makes N2 inactive as well. This can continue and form an inactive chain of neurons. Therefore, recognizing inactive neurons can help to detect weakly active or inactive zones of the brain. In addition, it can also help to simplify the structure of a neural network by removing such neurons from the network. In Section 5.5, we state this property for multiple input neurons.

5.4 The Spike Decreasing Property

The spike decreasing property is another property that shows a single input neuron cannot produce more 1s than the number of 1s in its input sequence. For example, if the input sequence is 11100110101, which means it contains seven 1s, the output of the neuron has less than or equal to 7 number of 1s. This property can easily be verified because, as proved earlier in Property 3, a single input neuron has either the delayer effect or the filter effect. A delayer neuron just repeats its input sequence. Thus, its output has the same number of 1s as its input sequence. A neuron with the filter effect produces 1 in its output for some number of 1s in its input. For example, for the input sequence above 11100110101 a 1/3 filter neuron produces 00100000100. So, neurons that have the filter effect contain fewer 1s in their output than in their input sequence. This property is stated as Property 5.

Property 5. $\forall\,(N: neuron)\,(input: list\,nat),$

$$Bin\_List(input) \land length\big(w(N)\big) = 1 \rightarrow count(input, 1) \geq count(Output(N'), 1)$$

In this property, $count$ is a function that calculates the number of occurrences of the number given as the second argument in the list given as the first argument. So, $count(input, 1)$ returns the number of 1s in the $input$ list and $count(Output(N'), 1)$ computes the number of 1s in the output list of the neuron N'. Recall that here N' is the neuron after initializing N and then applying all the inputs in the $input$ list. This property sounds trivial but guarantees a biological neuron cannot self-activate. Although, this property seems simple, a lemma is needed to prove it. The following lemma expresses that when a single input neuron receives a 0 as input, it cannot produce 1 in the output as follows.

Lemma 2. $\forall\,(N: neuron)\,(input: list\,nat),$

$$length\big(w(N)\big) = 1 \land input = [0] \rightarrow last\big(Output(N')\big) = 0$$

In the statement of this lemma, $last$ represents the last element of the given list, which is $Output(N')$ here. N' represents the neuron obtained from N by processing a single 0 as the next input. In other words, N' is obtained from N by a single application of NextNeuron without first applying ResetNeuron. Thus, $p(N')$ represents the value used to calculate $last\big(Output(N')\big)$, which is the last output value of the neuron.

Proof *(of Lemma 2).* The proof of this lemma is a straightforward consequence of Equation (1) in Definition 1.

Since the input of N is a single 0, we know from Definition 1 that $p(N') = w_1(N) \cdot 0$ or $p(N') = w_1(N) \cdot 0 + r(N) \cdot p(N)$. Simplifying the multipication by 0, we have these two cases:

$$p(N') = w_1(N) \cdot 0 = 0 \text{ or } p(N') = w_1(N) \cdot 0 + r(N) \cdot p(N) = r(N) \cdot p(N)$$

We know that $\tau(N') = \tau(N) > 0$. Thus, in the first case, $p(N') = 0 < \tau(N')$. According to Equation (2) in Definition 1, the next output of the neuron is 0 because its potential value $p(N')$ is less than its activation threshold $\tau(N')$. In the second case, when $p(N') = r(N) \cdot p(N)$, we know that $p(N) < \tau(N) = \tau(N')$ because of the condition of Equation (1) in Definition 1. Also, for every neuron, the leak factor is between 0 and 1. In other words, $0 \leq r(N) = r(N') \leq 1$. If $p(N) < 0$, multiplying it by a positive number produces a negative value which is less than $\tau(N)$. So, $p(N') = r(N) \cdot p(N) < 0 < \tau(N) = \tau(N')$. On the other hand, if $p(N) \geq 0$, multiplying it by a number between 0 and 1, produces a smaller number. So, $p(N') = r(N) \cdot p(N) < p(N) < \tau(N) = \tau(N')$. As can be seen, $p(N') < \tau(N')$ in this case also and thus the next output of the neuron is 0.

This completes the proof.

Now, we can use this lemma to prove Property 5.

Proof *(of Property 5)*. The proof is by induction on the length of the input sequence as follows.

Base case: $input = []$. If there is no input in the input sequence, the neuron will keep its initial status, i.e., $N = N'$. So, $Output(N') = [0]$. Therefore, $count(input, 1) = count([], 1) = 0 \geq count(Output(N'), 1) = 0$.

Induction case: We assume that the property is true for *input* and we must show that it holds for some *input'* of the form $(input + [h])$ for some additional input value h. Let N' be the neuron resulting from processing *input*, and let N'' be the neuron after processing *input'*. By the induction hypothesis, we know $count(input, 1) \geq count(Output(N'), 1)$ and we must prove that $count(input', 1) \geq count(Output(N''), 1)$.

Because *input'* is a binary list, we know that $h = 0$ or $h = 1$. We break this into two different cases, depending on the value of h.

First, we assume that $input' = input + [0]$. Because 0 is added to the *input* list, we have $count(input', 1) = count(input, 1)$. According to Lemma 2, that we just proved, having 0 as the last input in *input'* cannot produce 1 as the last output in the output list. So, we can conclude that $Output(N'') = Output(N') + [0]$. Similarly, because 0 is added to the output, $count(Output(N''), 1) = count(Output(N'), 1)$. Therefore,

$$count(input', 1) = count(input, 1) \geq count(Output(N'), 1) = count(Output(N''), 1).$$

Second, we assume that $input' = input + [1]$. In this case, 1 is added to the input list. Because the number of 1s is increased, it is not important that this new input produce 0 or 1 in the output list. The number of 1s in the output list remains unchanged or increase by 1. So, $count(Output(N''), 1)$ is at most $count(Output(N'), 1) + 1$. Also, we know that $count(input', 1) = count(input + [1], 1) = count(input, 1) + 1$. By the induction hypothesis we know that, $count(input, 1) \geq count(Output(N'), 1)$. By adding 1 to both sides of the inequality, we have $count(input, 1) + 1 \geq count(Output(N'), 1) + 1$.

Therefore, $count(input, 1) + 1 = count(input', 1) \geq count(Output(N''), 1)$.

This completes the proof.

So far, we proved five properties about single input neurons. We also explained a possible biological meaning for each of them but single input neurons do not exist in the human neural network. The reason we start with these neurons and state properties about them is that these properties can be used later to prove more complicated properties. In other words, these can be considered as the foundation of properties that we are going to prove later for multiple input neurons and archetypes. The biological meanings we stated for each of them can be extended easily as well. For example, the inhibitor effect says a single input neuron whose input weight is negative cannot create a spike in its output. In the next section, we extend this property for multiple input neurons. These properties are also useful to prove that the LI&F model has been correctly encoded in Coq (validation of the model with respect to key properties of the LI&F model).

5.5 The Inhibitor Effect for Multiple Input Neurons

In this section, we prove the inhibitor effect for multiple input neurons. We proved this property in Section 5.3 for single input neurons in Property 4. Since this is the first property we prove for neurons with multiple inputs, we need a new notation. To have a better understanding of the input sequence for a neuron with more than one input, before stating the property mathematically, we demonstrate the input sequence in Coq for multiple input neurons. Recall that for single input neurons, we use a binary list where the element of the list at index t represents the input of the neuron at time t. For multiple input neurons, each element of the input sequence is a binary list itself. For example, the input sequence of a neuron with 3 inputs can be `[[1;1;0]; [0;0;1]; [1;0;0]; [0;1;1]]`, which denotes that the input of the neuron at time 0 is `[1;1;0]`, it is `[1;0;0]` at time 1, `[1;0;0]` at time 2, and `[0;1;1]` at time 3. Now, we can express the inhibitor effect for multiple input neurons as stated below.

Property 6. $\forall\ (N\!:neuron)\ (t,\ n\!:nat)\ (\ell_1, \ell_2, ..., \ell_t\!:list\ nat),$

$$\left(\forall i, 1 \le i \le t, \ell_i = \left[x_1^i,\ x_2^i, ..., x_n^i\right] \wedge Bin\_List(\ell_i)\right) \wedge length\big(w(N)\big) = n\ \wedge$$

$$\left(\forall j, 1 \le j \le n,\ w_j(N) < 0\right) \rightarrow 1 \notin Output(N')$$

Property 6 is stated generally for neurons having any number n of inputs. The lists $\ell_1, \ell_2, ..., \ell_t$ each contain n values for the n inputs at each of the t time steps. In other words, the whole input sequence of the neuron N can be represented as $[\ell_1, \ell_2, ..., \ell_t]$ like we did in the Coq example above. Again, we write N' to denote the neuron obtained from initializing N and applying all ℓs in the sequence one by one. Thus, $p(N')$ represents the potential value after processing all inputs.

Proof *(of Property 6)*. The proof is by induction on t.

Base case: $t = 0$. If there is no input sequence, the neuron will keep its initial status, i.e., $N = N'$. So, $Output(N') = [0]$. Therefore, $1 \notin Output(N') = [0]$.

Induction case: We assume that the property holds for $t - 1$ and we show it holds for t. We know that $p(N')$ represents the potential value after initializing N and processing $\ell_1, \ell_2, ..., \ell_{t-1}$ one by one. We write N'' to denote the neuron obtained from initializing N and applying $\ell_1, \ell_2, ..., \ell_{t-1}, \ell_t$. In other words, N'' is N' after applying ℓ_t. By the induction hypothesis, we know $1 \notin Output(N')$ and we must prove that $1 \notin Output(N'')$.

Note that t is the time at which we produced the last output of N''. So, $p(N'')$ corresponds to $p(t)$ and $p(N')$ corresponds to $p(t - 1)$. Again, note that $\tau(N) = \tau(N') = \tau(N'')$ and similar equalities hold for r and w_js for all $1 \le j \le n$, so we use them interchangeably.

By the induction hypothesis, we know that $1 \notin Output(N')$, which means all values in the output of N' are 0, including the last one. According to Equation (2), because the last output of N' is 0, then $p(N') < \tau(N)$. According to Equation (1) and because $p(N') < \tau(N)$, we can conclude that $p(N'') = \sum_{j=1}^{n} x_j^t \cdot w_j(N) + r(N) \cdot p(N')$. We can expand the sum and write

$$p(N'') = x_1^t \cdot w_1(N) + x_2^t \cdot w_2(N) + \cdots + x_n^t \cdot w_n(N) + r(N) \cdot p(N')$$

Because for every i, $Bin\_List(\downarrow)$ and $\downarrow = [x_1^i, x_2^i, ..., x_n^i]$, we know that for every j, $x_j^t = 0$ or $x_j^t = 1$. Therefore, $x_j^t \cdot w_j(N) = 0$ or $x_j^t \cdot w_j(N) = w_j(N)$. Knowing that for every j, $w_j(N) < 0$, we can conclude that $x_j^t \cdot w_j(N) \leq 0$. This means if we sum all these $x_j^t \cdot w_j(N) \leq 0$, the sum will be less than or equal to 0, thus $\sum_{j=1}^{n} x_j^t \cdot w_j(N) \leq 0$.

Also, we know that $0 \leq r(N) \leq 1$ and considering that $p(N') < \tau(N)$, we can conclude that $r(N) \cdot p(N') < \tau(N)$ because if $p(N') \leq 0$, then $r(N) \cdot p(N') \leq 0 < \tau(N)$ and if $p(N') > 0$, $r(N) \cdot p(N') \leq p(N') < \tau(N)$. Recall that the activation threshold of a neuron is always positive, namely $0 < \tau(N)$ and multiplying a positive number by a number between 0 and 1, makes the result less than that number, thus $r(N) \cdot p(N') \leq p(N')$.

Putting these two together, we know that $\sum_{j=1}^{n} x_j^t \cdot w_j(N) \leq 0$ and $r(N) \cdot p(N') \leq 0 < \tau(N)$ and by adding both sides of these inequalities, we can conclude that $p(N'') = \sum_{j=1}^{n} x_j^t \cdot w_j(N) + r(N) \cdot p(N') < \tau(N)$. According to Equation (2), this means the next produced output after applying $\downarrow$ is 0 because $p(N'') < \tau(N)$, which means $1 \notin Output(N'')$.

This completes the proof.

5.6 Coq Implementation

We proved five properties about single-input neurons. We are going to show their Coq representation in this section. The Coq statements of Lemma 1, Property 1, Property 2, and Property 3 are shown in Figure 29. Lemma 1, Property 1, Property 2, and Property 3, called `AlwaysPos`, `Delayer_Property`, `Filter_Property`, and `DelayerOrFilterEffect` respectively. Note that these are statements of these lemmas and properties without their proofs.

```
Lemma AlwaysPos: forall (l: list nat) (N: Neuron),
      beq_nat (length (Weights N)) 1%nat = true /\
      Qle_bool 0 (hd 0 (Weights N)) = true
      -> Qle_bool 0 (Current (AfterNsteps (ResetNeuron N) l)) = true.

Theorem DelayerProperty: forall (Inputs: list nat) (N M: Neuron),
      beq_nat (length (Weights N)) 1%nat = true /\
      Eq_Neuron2 M (AfterNsteps (ResetNeuron N) Inputs) /\
      Bin_List Inputs /\ Qle_bool (Tau N) (hd 0 (Weights N)) = true
      -> Delayer_Effect Inputs (Output M).

Theorem FilterProperty: forall (Inputs: list nat) (N M: Neuron),
      beq_nat (length (Weights N)) 1%nat = true /\
      Eq_Neuron2 M (AfterNsteps (ResetNeuron N) Inputs) /\
      Bin_List Inputs /\ Qle_bool (Tau N) (hd 0 (Weights N)) = false /\
      Inputs <> nil -> (Filter_Effect (Output M)).

Theorem DelayerOrFilterEffect: forall (Inputs: list nat) (N M: Neuron),
      beq_nat (length (Weights N)) 1%nat = true /\
      Eq_Neuron2 M (AfterNsteps (ResetNeuron N) Inputs) /\
      Bin_List Inputs ->
      (Delayer_Effect Inputs (Output M)) \/ (Filter_Effect Inputs (Output M)).
```

Figure 29. Statement of Lemma 1, Property 1, Property 2, and Property 3 in Coq

Recall that `AlwaysPos` states that the membrane potential of a single input neuron, whose only input weights is non-negative, is always non-negative and we use it in the proof of `Delayer_Property`.

```
Lemma ZeroInputZeroOutput: forall (N: Neuron) (Inputs: list nat),
        beq_nat (length (Weights N)) 1%nat = true /\
        beq_nat (length Inputs) 1%nat = true /\
        beq_nat (hd 0%nat (Weights N)) 0%nat = true
        -> beq_nat (NextOutput N Inputs) 0%nat = true.

Theorem NegativeWeight: forall (Inputs: list nat) (N M: Neuron),
        beq_nat (length (Weights N)) 1%nat = true /\
        Qlt_bool (hd 0 (Weights N)) 0 = true /\
        Eq_Neuron2 M (AfterNsteps (ResetNeuron N) Inputs) /\
        Bin_List Inputs
        -> ~ (In 1%nat (Output M)).

Theorem SpikeDecreasing: forall (Inputs: list nat) (N M: Neuron),
        beq_nat (length (Weights N)) 1%nat = true /\
        Eq_Neuron2 M (AfterNsteps (ResetNeuron N) Inputs) /\
        Bin_List Inputs
        -> (count (Output M) 1%nat) <=? (count Inputs 1%nat).
```

Figure 30. Statement of Lemma 2, Property 4, and Property 5 in Coq

The Coq statement of Lemma 2, Property 4, Property 5, and Property 6 are shown in Figure 30. Lemma 2, Property 4, and Property 5, are called `ZeroInputZeroOutput`, `NegativeWeight`, and `SpikeDecreasing` respectively. Property 4 demonstrates a special case about the archetype in Figure 2(e).

There are some functions in the statements of these lemmas and theorems in Figure 29 and Figure 30, that require explanation. `Eq_Neuron2` checks if two neurons are equal. For two neurons to be equal, all data fields have to be equal. For equality, record constraints are not required to be checked. The definition of this function is shown in Figure 31. Note that == is the equality defined for rational numbers in the Coq library and = is Coq standard equality operator, used here on lists.

```
Definition Eq_Neuron2 (N: Neuron) (M: Neuron): Prop :=
  (Output N) = (Output M) /\
  (Weights N) = (Weights M) /\
  (Leak_Factor N) == (Leak_Factor M) /\
  (Tau N) == (Tau M) /\
  (Current N) == (Current M).
```

Figure 31. Definition of `Eq_Neuron2` for checking equality of two neurons

Another useful function here is `AfterNsteps`, which applies a list of n inputs to a neuron and returns the neuron after processing all of those inputs by that neuron. The definition of this function is shown in Figure 32. Note that it applies `NextNeuron` defined earlier in Figure 26. In the statements of properties, `AfterNsteps` is applied to a neuron after it is initialized using the function `ResetNeuron`, which was also stated earlier in Figure 28. This is because in all properties we proved, we start from the initial state of a neuron.

```
Fixpoint AfterNsteps (N: Neuron) (Inputs: list nat): Neuron :=
  match Inputs with
  | nil => N
  | h::t => NextNeuron (AfterNsteps N t) [h]
  end.
```

Figure 32. Definition of `AfterNsteps` for returning a neuron after applying an input list

In the statement of Property 1, `Delayer_Effect`, which is shown in Figure 33, is a predicate that represents when two lists are related by the delayer effect property. For example, if the first list is `[0;1;1]` and the second list is `[0;1;1;0]`, this predicate is equivalent to `True`. Recall that we keep the output list of a neuron in reverse order to make proofs by induction easier. This means that the head of the list is the most recent output of the neuron. Therefore, in the example above, the input list represents 110 and the output list represents 0110 which is the same as the input with a delay of 0 at the beginning. If two lists are not related in this way, the predicate is equivalent to `False`. Recall that in the definition of `Delayer_Effect`, the function `beq_nat`, which is shown in Figure 15, is a function that checks the equality of two natural numbers.

```
Fixpoint Delayer_Effect (In: list nat) (Out: list nat): Prop :=
  match In with
    | nil => match Out with
               | nil => False
               | h2::t2 => (beq_nat h2 0%nat) = true /\ t2 = nil
             end
    | h1::t1 => match Out with
               | nil => False
               | h2::t2 => (beq_nat h1 h2) = true /\ (Delayer_Effect t1 t2)
             end
  end.
```

Figure 33. Definition of `Delayer_Effect` for checking the delayer effect between two lists

In the statement of **Property 2**, `Filter_Effect` is a predicate that expresses when a list has the filter effect property, which means there are no two consecutive ones in the list. For example, if the argument list is $[0;1;0;0;1;0]$, this predicate holds and if the list is $[0;1;0;1;1;0]$, it does not hold. The filter effect only applies to lists of length 2 or more.

```
Fixpoint Filter_Effect (Out: list nat): Prop :=
  match Out with
    | nil => False
    | h1::t1 => match t1 with
               | nil => False
               | h2::t2 => match t2 with
                          | nil => (beq_nat h1 0%nat) = true /\ (beq_nat h2 0%nat) = true
                          | h3::t3 => if (beq_nat h1 0%nat)
                                      then Filter_Effect t1
                                      else (beq_nat h2 0%nat) = true /\ Filter_Effect t1
                        end
             end
  end.
```

Figure 34. Definition of `Filter_Effect` for checking the filter effect of a list

Furthermore, lists of length 2 can only contain 0 because a single input neuron has 0 in its output in the initial state and when its input weight is less than its activation threshold, the second output is 0. That is why `Filter_Effect` does not hold when the length of its argument is less than 1.

Note that the result of checking for consecutive ones is the same for a list and its reverse. `Filter_Effect` is shown in Figure 34.

```
Theorem SpikeDecreasing: forall (Out Inputs: list nat) (N M: Neuron),
        beq_nat (length (Weights N)) 1%nat = true /\
        Eq_Neuron2 M (AfterNsteps (ResetNeuron N) Inputs) /\
        Bin_List Inputs
        -> (count (Output M) 1%nat) <=? (count Inputs 1%nat).
Proof.
  induction Inputs as [| h l].
  - intros. inversion H as [H1 [H2 H3]]. simpl in H2. unfold Eq_Neuron2 in H2.
    inversion H2 as [H4 [H5 [H6 [H7 H8]]]]. simpl in H4. rewrite H4. simpl.
    reflexivity.
  - intros. inversion H as [H1 [H2 H3]]. simpl in H3. inversion H3 as [H4 H5].
    unfold Eq_Neuron2 in H2. inversion H2 as [H6 [H7 [H8 [H9 H10]]]].
    simpl in H7. simpl in H8. simpl in H9. simpl in H10. simpl in H6.
    remember (AfterNsteps (ResetNeuron N) l) as M2.
    assert (Htemp: (length (Weights N) =? 1) = true /\
    Eq_Neuron2 M2 (AfterNsteps (ResetNeuron N) l) /\ Bin_List l).
    { split. apply H. split. rewrite <- HeqM2. unfold Eq_Neuron2. simpl. split.
      reflexivity. split. reflexivity. split. reflexivity. split; reflexivity.
      apply H5. } generalize (IH1 N M2); intro H1. apply H1 in Htemp.
    destruct (h =? 0) eqn: HBN.
    + rewrite beq_nat_true_iff in HBN. rewrite HBN. simpl.
      assert (HLen: (length (Weights M2) =? 1) = true).
      { generalize (Unchanged (ResetNeuron N) l); intro HRM.
        inversion HRM as [HRM1 [HRM2 HRM3]]. generalize (ResetUnchanged N);
        intro HR. inversion HR as [HR1 [HR2 HR3]]. rewrite <- HR3 in HRM3.
        rewrite <- HeqM2 in HRM3. rewrite HRM3 in H1. auto. }
      generalize (ZeroInputZeroOutput M2 [0%nat]); intro HZM. apply HZM in HLen.
      rewrite HBN in H6. rewrite beq_nat_true_iff in HLen. rewrite HLen in H6.
      rewrite H6. simpl. auto. auto. auto.
    + simpl in H4. rewrite beq_nat_true_iff in H4. rewrite H4.
      generalize (NextOutput01 M2 [h]); intro HNAR. inversion HNAR as [HN1 | HN2].
      * rewrite beq_nat_true_iff in HN1. rewrite HN1 in H6. rewrite H6. simpl.
        rewrite <- HN1 in H6. generalize (LeqSucc (count l 1)); intro HLC.
        generalize (LeqAssociativity
              (count (Output M2) 1) (count l 1) (S (count l 1))); intro HLA.
        apply HLA in Htemp. auto. auto.
      * rewrite beq_nat_true_iff in HN2. rewrite HN2 in H6. rewrite H6. simpl.
        auto.
Qed.
```

Figure 35. Detailed proof of the `SpikDecreasing` property in Coq

In the statement of Property 4, which is called `NegativeWeight` in the Coq code, `In` is a predicate in the list library of Coq that checks if an element belongs to a list. Recall that ~ is an operator for logical not. Thus, `~(In 1%nat (Output M))` expresses that there is no 1 in the output list of neuron `M`. We recall here that in the statement of Property 5, which is called `SpikeDecreasing` in Coq, `count` is a Coq library function that calculates the number of occurrences of a given element in a given list. For example, `(count Inputs 1%nat)` returns the number of the element 1 in the list `Inputs`. Proofs of these properties and lemmas in Coq are pretty long because we need to use a lot of tactics to guide the proof assistant through. Verifications of proofs are usually more difficult and longer than their mathematical versions. This is because some mathematical facts and theorems are clearer for a human reader than the proof assistant.

```
Fixpoint AllNegative (l: list Q): Prop :=
  match l with
    | nil => True
    | h::t => h < 0 /\ AllBinary t
  end.

Fixpoint AllBinary (Inputs: list (list nat)): Prop :=
  match Inputs with
    | nil => True
    | h::t => Bin_List h /\ AllBinary t
  end.

Fixpoint AllLengthN (Inputs: list (list nat)) (n: nat) : Prop :=
  match Inputs with
    | nil => True
    | h::t => (beq_nat n (length h)) = true /\ AllLengthN t
  end.

Fixpoint AfterNstepsM (N: Neuron) (Inputs: list (list nat)): Neuron :=
  match Inputs with
    | nil => N
    | h::t => NextNeuron (AfterNstepsM N t) h
  end.

Theorem MultipleNegativeWeight:
        forall (Inputs: list (list nat)) (n: nat) (N M: Neuron),
        beq_nat (length (Weights N)) n = true /\
        AllLengthN Inputs n /\
        AllBinary Inputs /\
        AllNegative (Weights N) /\
        Eq_Neuron2 M (AfterNstepsM (ResetNeuron N) Inputs)
        -> ~(In 1%nat (Output M)).
```

Figure 36. The definition of Property 6 in Coq and needed helper functions for its statement

Just as an example here, we present the proof of the `SpikeDecreasing` property in Figure 35, which is relatively shorter than the other proofs. Proofs of other properties are available in our accompanying Coq code. Recall that we use lemma `ZeroInputZeroOutput`, which states that when the input of a single input neuron is 0, its output is 0, in the proof of `SpikeDecreasing`.

We show this Coq proof for illustration purposes. Note that this proof uses tactics such as `intros`, `destruct`, `rewrite`, and `induction`, which are described in Chapter 3. It also uses other basic Coq tactics such as `apply`, `generalize`, `split`, `auto`, etc. Definitions of some built-in and some defined lemmas are not presented in Figure 35. They can be found in the Coq library or in our accompanying Coq code.

Finally, we present the statement of Property 6, which is called `MultipleNegativeWeight`. Recall that this property states that a neuron whose input weights are all negative cannot produce 1 in its output. This property is shown in Figure 36 alongside with the definitions of four helper functions that are needed to state the property.

In the definition of `MultipleNegativeWeight` shown in Figure 36, `Inputs` has the type `(list (list nat))`. We mentioned an example of such a list in Section 5.5, namely `[[1;1;0]; [0;0;1]; [1;0;0]; [0;1;1]]`. The assumption `beq_nat (length (Weights N)) n = true` expresses that the number of inputs of the neuron `N`, which is a multiple input neuron, is n. The predicate `AllLengthN Inputs n` is true when all lists in the list `Inputs` has length n and false otherwise. Recall that each element of `Inputs` is the list of inputs of neuron `N` at a certain time step. The predicate `AllBinary Inputs` is true when all lists in the list `Inputs` are binary lists and false otherwise. Note that in Figure 36, this predicate uses the predicate `Bin_List` shown in Figure 21 to check that each element of `Inputs` is a binary list. Finally, the predicate `AllNegative (Weight N)` is true when all input weights of neuron `N`, namely all elements of the list `(Weight N)` are negative. The function `AfterNstepsM` does the same job as the function `AfterNsteps` shown in Figure 32 but for multiple input neurons. In other words, `AfterNstepsM` applies all list of inputs in `Inputs` to neuron `N` after initializing it using the `ResetNeuron` function. The conclusion of this property is the same as the property `NegativeWeight` shown in Figure 30, namely `~(In 1%nat (Output M))`, which states that there is no spike in the output of the neuron `M`, which is the result of applying all input lists in `Inputs` to the initialized version of the neuron N, namely `(ResetNeuron N)`. The verification of this property is left as future work for this book.

Chapter 6

Definition of Archetypes and Their Properties in Coq

As mentioned earlier, archetypes can be considered as the smallest unit of neural networks after neurons. Each archetype consists of two or more neurons. They perform functions of neural networks. More precisely, our body is controlled by the central processing unit of the body, which is our neural network. The neural network can organize and order some actions such as breathing, walking, touching, smelling, tasting, etc. Each of these actions are generated by functional structures in our brain and each of them consists of many archetypes. These archetypes' jobs are as simple as communicating, transferring signals, amplifying signals, repeating signals, etc. In this chapter of the book, first in Section 6.1, we discuss the definition of archetypes. Then, in Section 6.2, we introduce the archetype for a series of delayer neurons and in Section 6.3 we prove a property about this archetype, which can produce delays in an input signal. In Section 6.4, we introduce the positive loop archetype and in Section 6.5, we prove two properties about this archetype, which can create a persistent sequence of 1s in its output. In Section 6.6 and Section 6.7, we introduce the negative loop archetype and the contralateral inhibition archetype and state a property for each of them.

6.1 Definition of Archetypes in Coq

Similar to the neuron definition, we use records to define archetypes. The difference here is we have many archetypes and each of them needs its own definition. When using Coq records, we have to be careful about field names. For example, if we need to define two archetypes A1 and A2 and each of them has two neurons, we cannot us the names, N1 and N2 for the neuron fields in A2 if these names have already been used for the neurons in A1. Although, this is quite normal in regular programming languages, it is not allowed in Coq. This problem can be solved by naming neuron fields of A1, N1_A1 and N2_A1 and naming neuron fields of A2, N1_A2 and N2_A2. This will be seen in the definition of archetypes later in this chapter. As mentioned earlier, records in Coq can receive inputs and build their fields based on the given inputs. For every input to a record, a new instance of the record is created. For instance, if REC is a defined record that takes a list of natural number called as a parameter, then if L1 and L2 are two different lists of natural numbers, then (REC L1) and (REC L2) are two instances of REC. Like the record for the definition of neurons shown in Figure 20, parameterized records that we use for the definition of archetypes can have constraints. These constraints can be defined on the parameter of the record or on its fields or both. We start with the definition of our archetypes in the next section of this chapter.

6.2 Series of Single-Input Neurons

The first archetype that we introduce is a series of single-input neurons. This archetype is shown in Figure 2(a). In the structure of this archetype, the first neuron receives an input from the outside. Starting from the second neuron, each neuron receives its input from the previous neuron and sends its output to the next neuron. The output of the last neuron is the output of the archetype. This archetype is defined in Coq as shown in Figure 37.

```
Record NeuronSeries {Input: list nat} := MakeNeuronSeries
{
        NeuronList: list Neuron;
        NSOutput: list nat;
        AllSingle: forall (N:Neuron),
            In N NeuronList -> (beq_nat (length (Weights N)) 1%nat) = true;
        SeriesOutput: NSOutput = (SeriesNetworkOutput Input NeuronList);
}.
```

Figure 37. Definition of `NeuronSeries` archetype

This record has two data fields and two constraints. The first data field is a list of neurons called `NeuronList` that stores all neurons in the series. As in previous definitions, we keep the list of neurons backward, which means the head of the list contains the last neuron in the series and the last element in this list is the first neuron in the series. The second data field is a list of natural numbers called `NSOutput`, which saves the output of the series, which is the output list of the last neuron in the series. The last neuron is the head of `NeuronList`. The first constraint of this archetype, which is called `AllSingle`, says that every neuron in the series is a single-input neuron. More precisely, if N is a member of `Neuronlist`, expressed using the predicate `In`, the length of the weight list of that neuron is 1. Recall that `beq_nat` checks equality of natural numbers and returns a Boolean. As can be seen in Figure 37, this record takes a list of natural numbers as input. This list is the list of inputs that are going to be fed to the first neuron in the series one by one. Recall that we also keep this list backward. So, the head of the list is the last input that is sent to the first neuron in the series. Thus, both `NeuronList` and `Input` are kept in reverse order. The second constraint in this archetype, which is called `SeriesOutput`, relates the output of the series to its input and the `NeruonList` using a function called `SeriesNetworkOutput` for this purpose. The definition of `SeriesNetworkOutput` is shown in Figure 38.

```
Fixpoint SeriesNetworkOutput (Input: list nat)

                             (NeuronList: list Neuron): (list nat) :=

match NeuronList with

| nil => Input

| h::t => (Output (AfterNsteps (ResetNeuron h) (SeriesNetworkOutput Input t)))

end.
```

Figure 38. Definition of `SeriesNetworkOutput` function

`SeriesNetworkOutput` takes the input list of the neuron and the list of neurons in the series and applies each input in the input list one by one to the series using `AfterNSteps`, which is described in Chapter 5 in Figure 32.

6.3 The Delayer Effect in a Series of Single-Input Neurons

The first property that we consider about an archetype is the *delayer effect* in a *series of single-input* neurons. Recall that in the series archetype, each neuron output is the input of the next neuron. If we have a series of n single input neurons and all of them have the delayer effect, then the output of the whole structure is the input plus n leading zeros. For example, if the input is 10010100111 then the output of such a series with 5 neurons that are delayers will be 0000010010100111. In other words, this structure transfers the input sequence exactly with a delay marked by the n leading zeros, denoted as $zeros(n)$ in the statement of the property below. This property is expressed as follows.

Property 7. $\forall \, (input: list\ nat) \, \big(NSeries: (NeuronSeries\ input)\big) \, (i: nat),$

$$length\big(NeuronList(NSeries)\big) = n \wedge Bin\_List(input) \wedge$$

$$\begin{pmatrix} \forall i \ 0 \leq i < n, & length\big(w(NeuronList(NSeries)[i])\big) = 1 \wedge \\ w_1(NeuronList(NSeries)[i]) > \tau(NeuronList(NSeries)[i]) \end{pmatrix} \rightarrow$$

$$NSOutput(NSeries) = zeros(n) + input$$

Proof *(of Property 7)*. Note that *NSeries* is an instantiated record of the archetype *NSeries* defined in Figure 37 by applying *NeuronSeries* to the list of natural numbers *input* and *NeuronList(NSeries)* refers to the list of neurons in this archetype. *NeuronList(NSeries)[i]* represents the i-th neuron in this list. The assumption
$$\left(\begin{array}{l} \forall i\ 0 \le i < n,\ length\big(w(NeuronList(NSeries)[i])\big) = 1 \wedge \\ w_1(NeuronList(NSeries)[i]) > \tau(NeuronList(NSeries)[i]) \end{array} \right)$$
expresses that all neurons in *NeuronList(NSeries)* are delayers (See the assumption of Property 1). Here for simplicity in writing the proof, we write *Series* to denote *NeuronList(NSeries)*, which is the first field of the record in Figure 37. So, *Series[i]* denotes the i-th neuron in the *Series*. This time we need to use induction on the length of *Series*. In the property statement, $zeros(m)$ means a sequence of 0s of length m. Also, *NSOutput(NSeries)* denotes the final output of the series structure which is equal to *Output(Series[n])*. In this proof, we simply use *NSOutput* to refer to *NSOutput(NSeries)*.

Base case: $n = 1$. In this case, there is only one neuron in the series and we know that this neuron has the delayer effect. According to Property 1 proved in Chapter 5, we can conclude that $NSOutput = [0] + input + [0] = zeros(1) + input$.

Induction case: We assume that the property holds for *Series* of length k. Let $NSOutput'$ be the output of this series. Thus, by the induction hypothesis, $NSOutput' = zeros(k) + input$. We must show that the property holds for a $Series + [M]$, where M is a neuron such that $length\big(w(M)\big) = 1$ and $w_1(M) > \tau(M)$. Let $NSOutput''$ be the output of this series of length $k + 1$. The input sequence for M is the final output of *Series*, which is $zeros(k) + input$. By the assumptions of this property, all neurons in $Series + [M]$ satisfy Property 1, i.e., have the delayer effect, including the last one M, which means that its output is equal to its input plus a leading 0. In other words, $NSOutput'' = [0] + zeros(k) + input$. Therefore, we can conclude that $NSOutput'' = [0] + zeros(k) + input = zeros(k + 1) + input$.

This completes the proof.

As mentioned earlier, we can guarantee that the properties we prove are true in the general case, such as true for any input values, any length of input, and any amount of time. As an example, this property is called simple series in [27]. The authors were able to write a function (more precisely, a Lustre node), which encodes the expected behavior of the simple series in [27]. Then, they could call a model checker to test whether the property at issue is valid for some input series with a fixed length. In Property 7, we proved that the desired behavior is true for any length and any parameters of the series. The statement of this property in Coq is shown in Figure 39. It is called `SeriesN` in Coq.

```
Theorem SeriesN: forall (Input: list nat) (NSeries: @NeuronSeries Input),
    AllDelayers (NeuronList NSeries) ->
    Bin_List Input ->
    (NSOutput NSeries) = Input ++ (NZeros (length (NeuronList NSeries))).
```

Figure 39. Statement of `SeriesN` for the delayer effect of series of single input neurons

In this property, `NSeries` is name of the record `NeuronSeries` instantiated with `Input`, which is a list of natural numbers and the first argument of this theorem. (`NSOutput NSeries`) denotes the field `NSOutput` of `NSeries`, which is the output of the series. In the previous properties, we used `/\` to express the assumptions of the theorem as a conjunction. Here we use implication `->` instead of `/\`. This comes from the fact that `A /\ B /\ C -> R` is the logical equivalent of `A -> B -> C -> R`.

```
Fixpoint AllDelayers (NeuronList: list Neuron): Prop :=
  match NeuronList with
  | nil => True
  | h::t => (beq_nat (length (Weights h)) 1%nat) = true /\
            Qle_bool (Tau h) (hd 0 (Weights h)) = true /\
            AllDelayers t
  end.

Fixpoint NZeros (n: nat): list nat :=
  match n with
  | O => nil
  | S n' => 0%nat::NZeros n'
  end.
```

Figure 40. Definition of `AllDelayers` and `NZeros` functions in Coq

There are two helper functions used to express the statement of `SeriesN`, which are `AllDelayers` and `NZeros`. `AllDelayers` takes a list of neurons and is equivalent to `True` when all neurons in the list are delayers, which means they are single input neurons whose weights are greater than their thresholds, i.e. $w_1(Series[i]) > \tau(Series[i])$. `NZeros` takes an integer L and returns a list of length L whose elements are all 0s. Definitions of these two functions are shown in Figure 40.

```
Theorem SeriesN: forall (Input: list nat) (NSeries: @NeuronSeries Input),
    AllDelayers (NeuronList NSeries) ->
    Bin_List Input ->
    (NSOutput NSeries) = Input ++ (NZeros (length (NeuronList NSeries))).
Proof.
  intros Input NSeries.
  destruct NSeries.
  simpl. generalize dependent NSOutput0.
  induction NeuronList0 as [| h t].
  - simpl. rewrite app_nil_r. auto.
  - simpl; intros. inversion H as [H1 [H2 H3]]. clear H.
    assert (H: SeriesNetworkOutput Input t = SeriesNetworkOutput Input t).
    { auto. }
    assert
    (HAS: forall N: Neuron, In N t -> (beq_nat (length (Weights N)) 1%nat) = true).
    { generalize (AllSingleInput t H3); intro HAN. apply HAN. }
    generalize (IHt HAS (SeriesNetworkOutput Input t) H H3 H0).
    intro H4. clear H.
    rewrite SeriesOutput0. clear SeriesOutput0 NSOutput0.
    rewrite -> H4. clear H4.
    generalize (StillBin Input (length t)); intro HSB.
    apply HSB in H0.
    remember (AfterNsteps (ResetNeuron h) (Input ++ NZeros (length t))) as M.
    generalize (Delayer_Property (Input ++ NZeros (length t)) h M); intro HDP.
    assert (Htemp: (length (Weights h)) =? 1) = true /\
        Eq_Neuron2 M (AfterNsteps (ResetNeuron h) (Input ++ NZeros (length t))) /\
        Bin_List (Input ++ NZeros (length t)) /\
        Qle_bool (Tau h) (hd 0 (Weights h)) = true).
    { split; auto. split; auto. rewrite HeqM. unfold Eq_Neuron2.
      split; auto. split; auto. split; auto. reflexivity.
      split; auto. reflexivity. split; auto. }
    apply HDP in Htemp. apply Delayer_lists in Htemp. rewrite Htemp.
    rewrite <- app_assoc. rewrite AppendZero. reflexivity.
Qed.
```

Figure 41. The proof of Property 7 called `SeriesN` in Coq

In every proof assistant such as Coq, we can use the result of previously proved properties to prove some new properties. As mentioned in the mathematical proof of Property 7, we use Property 1 to conclude that the output of each neuron has a delay because we know all neurons in the series are delayers. In Coq, we can use previously proved properties via tactics such as `apply` and `generalize`. Using proved properties can make the proof of a new property significantly shorter. The Coq proof of Property 7 is shown in Figure 41. As can be seen in this proof, Property 1, which is called `Delayer_Property` in Coq, is applied using the `generalize` tactic.

6.4 The Definition of the Positive Loop Archetype

We introduce a new archetype in this section and prove an interesting property about it in the next section. This archetype is called a *two-neuron positive loop* or shortly a positive loop. This archetype is not shown in Figure 2 but it is a very close structure to the archetype in Figure 2(d), except that in the archetype in Figure 2(d), the second neuron inhibits the first neuron (recall that the filled black circle is a sign of negative weight or inhibition) while in the positive loop, the second neuron activates the first neuron. The structure of the positive loop is shown in Figure 42. In biology, the idea of a positive loop is simply having a system whose output amplifies the system itself. In other words, it allows us to amplify the input signal or extend it in time. It can also provoke a chain reaction. The biological system can use this archetype to activate itself up to reaching its maximum, without having the capability of leaving it. There are two neurons in this archetype. N1 has two inputs, one input is the input of the network. The other input comes from the output of N2. N2 is a single-input neuron whose input is the output of N1. The output of N2 is the output of the archetype.

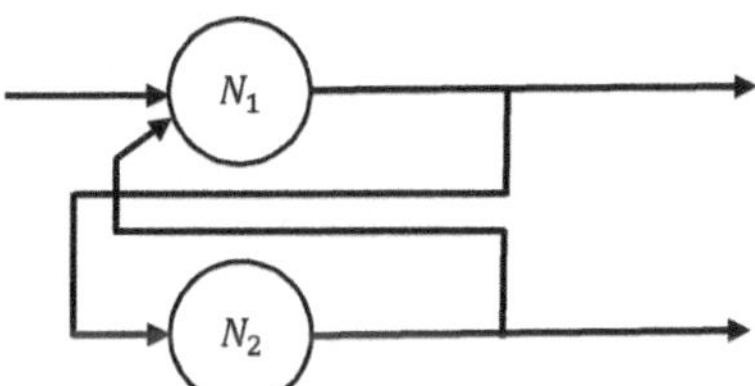

Figure 42. The two-neuron positive loop archetype

The first neuron in both the negative loop and the positive loop activates the second neuron. The difference with Figure 2(d) is that the arrow going into $N1$ from the output of $N2$ is not an inhibitor. Because it activates instead, it creates the amplification effect the we described earlier. We will explain the structure of the negative loop in the next section. The positive loop is defined in Coq in Figure 43. As can be seen in Figure 43, the positive loop is a parameterized record that takes a list of natural numbers as input and creates the record based on this input. This record has two fields, which represent the neurons N1 and N2 in the structure of the positive loop shown in Figure

41. They are called `PL_N1` and `PL_N2` here. We simply use `N1` and `N2` here to refer to `PL_N1` and `PL_N2`. The rest of the fields in this record are constraints.

```
Record PositiveLoop {Inputs: list nat} := MakePositiveLoop
{
  PL_N1: Neuron;
  PL_N2: Neuron;
  PL_NinputN1: (beq_nat (length (Weights PL_N1)) 2%nat) = true;
  PL_NinputN2: (beq_nat (length (Weights PL_N2)) 1%nat) = true;
  PL_PW1: 0 < (hd 0 (Weights PL_N1));
  PL_PW2: 0 < (hd 0 (tl (Weights PL_N1)));
  PL_PW3: 0 < (hd 0 (Weights PL_N2));
  PL_Connection1: Eq_Neuron2 PL_N1 (AfterNTwoLoopN1 (ResetNeuron PL_N1)
                  (ResetNeuron PL_N2) Inputs);
  PL_Connection2: Eq_Neuron2 PL_N2 (AfterNTwoLoopN2 (ResetNeuron PL_N1)
                  (ResetNeuron PL_N2) Inputs)
}.
```

Figure 43. Definition of the positive loop in Coq

The first and second constraints namely `PL_NinputN1` and `PL_NinputN2`, state the number of inputs for the neurons `N1` and `N2` respectively, which are 2 for `N1` and 1 for `N2`. The next three constraints namely, `PL_PW1`, `PL_PW2`, and `PL_PW3` express that all weights in this archetype are positive. Recall that `Weights` is the list of all input weights to a neuron. `PL_PW1` states that the head of this list for the neuron `N1` is positive. `PL_PW2` states that the head of the tail of `Weights` of the neuron `N1` is positive, which means the second input weight of this neuron is greater than 0. Finally, `PL_PW3` states that the head of `Weights` of the neuron `N2`, which is the only input weight of the neuron `N2` is positive. To explain the last two constraints, we need to describe the functions `AfterNTwoLoopN1` and `AfterNTwoLoopN2`.

These two functions are shown in Figure 44. `AfterNTwoLoopN1` takes two neurons and a list of natural numbers as inputs. The list of natural numbers is in fact a binary list and all elements of this list are applied as the first input of the first neuron respectively. The second input of the first neuron is the output of the second neuron and the only input of the second neuron is the output of the first neuron. This function returns the status of the first neuron after applying all inputs. `AfterNTwoLoopN2` performs almost the same operation except that this function returns the second neuron after applying all inputs to the archetype. As seen in Figure 44, the syntax for defining `AfterNTwoLoopN2` is different because of the fact that `AfterNTwoLoopN1` and

`AfterNTwoLoopN2` are mutually recursive. Recall that in programming languages, a function is simply recursive when it calls itself in the body of the function, but when functions call each other in a cycle, they are called mutually recursive. For example, function A calls function B, function B calls function C, and function C calls function A. The new syntax is needed because a function has to be defined before it gets called. In programming languages such as C, this problem is solved by writing the prototype of functions before their definitions. In Coq, we need to write it as shown in Figure 44, which means we write the definition of the first function in the loop, namely `AfterNTwoLoopN1`, which calls `AfterNTwoLoopN2` in its body and by using the keyword `with` we can write the definition of the second function in the loop which is `AfterNTwoLoopN2`. Then, `AfterNTwoLoopN2` can call `AfterNTwoLoopN1`. Note that the types of the inputs for `AfterNTwoLoopN2` are not written here because it uses the same arguments as `AfterNTwoLoopN1`. Types can be omitted in Coq when they can be inferred, we usually include them for readability.

```
Fixpoint AfterNTwoLoopN1 (N1 N2: Neuron) (Inputs: list nat): Neuron :=
  match Inputs with
  | nil => N1
  | h::t => NextNeuron (AfterNTwoLoopN1 N1 N2 t)
             [h; (hd 0%nat (Output (AfterNTwoLoopN2 N1 N2 t)))]
  end
with AfterNTwoLoopN2 N1 N2 Inputs :=
  match Inputs with
  | nil => N2
  | h::t => NextNeuron (AfterNTwoLoopN2 N1 N2 t)
             [(hd 0%nat (Output (AfterNTwoLoopN1 N1 N2 t)))]
  end.
```

Figure 44. Definition of `AfterNTwoLoopN1` and `AfterNTwoLoopN2` using indirect recursive

In Figure 43, the last two constraints show that the neuron N1 is equal to the output of the function `AfterNTwoLoopN1` and the neuron N2 is equal to the output of the function `AfterNTwoLoopN2` after applying all inputs in the list `Inputs` to the neuron N1. In the next section, we define and prove an interesting property about the positive loop archetype.

6.5 The Amplifier Property for the Positive Loop and its Proof

In this section, we introduce and prove an interesting property that shows the ability of the positive loop structure to amplify signals. As mentioned in the previous section, the positive loop can provide a system that can keep itself activated. In biology, these structures can create chain reactions, which can help us transfer signals while keeping them activated and prevent them from damping. A chain reaction in biology is a series of events where each one activates the next one. Here in the positive loop archetype, we are interested in creating a series of spikes by feeding a particular series of inputs to the first neuron. We call this property the *amplifier* property. It states that if the input list given to this archetype has the pattern $(011)^*$, both input weights of the first neuron are greater than or equal to its activation threshold, and the only input weight of the second neuron is greater than or equal to their activation thresholds, then starting at time 2, the first neuron only emits spikes. A direct corollary of this property is that the second neuron produces only 1 as output with a delay starting at time 3. This property is stated as follows.

Property 8. $\forall\ (Inputs: list\ nat)\ \big(PLP: (PositiveLoop\ Inputs)\big)\ (time: nat),$

$$w_1\big(PL\_N1(PLP)\big) \geq \tau\big(PL\_N1(PLP)\big) \wedge w_2\big(PL\_N1(PLP)\big) \geq \tau\big(PL\_N1(PLP)\big) \wedge$$

$$w_1\big(PL\_N2(PLP)\big) \geq \tau\big(PL\_N2(PLP)\big) \wedge Inputs = (011)^*(\varepsilon + 0 + 01) \wedge 1 < time \wedge$$

$$time < length\big(Output(PL\_N1(PLP))\big) \rightarrow Output(PL\_N1(PLP))[time] = 1$$

The biological meaning of this property is that, thanks to the positive loop, we are able to produce a persistent sequence of 1s starting from a periodic pattern containing a zero in the input (i.e., we can produce a sequence of 1s starting from a sequence that does not contain only 1s). It is a sort of self-excitation. In the statement of this property, *PLP* is an instance of the positive loop with the list of natural numbers *Inputs* as its argument. $PL\_N1(PLP)$ denotes the first neuron in the positive loop archetype and $PL\_N2(PLP)$ denotes the second neuron in this archetype. Recall that two records in Coq cannot have fields with the same name and that is why we named these two neurons in the record of the positive loop `PL_N1` and `PL_N2` but here in this proof, we simply use $N1$ instead of $PL\_N1(PLP)$ and $N2$ instead of $PL\_N2(PLP)$. Note that the constraints `PL_Connection1` and `PL_Connection2` in Figure 43 ensure that $Output(N1)$ and $Output(N2)$ represent the outputs of these two neurons given the *Inputs* as the parameter of the positive loop archetype. The assumptions $w_1\big(PL\_N1(PLP)\big) \geq \tau\big(PL\_N1(PLP)\big)$ and $w_2\big(PL\_N1(PLP)\big) \geq \tau\big(PL\_N1(PLP)\big)$ simply indicate that both inputs of the neuron $N1$ are greater than or equal to their thresholds. In other words, if one of the inputs of $N1$ is 1, then this neuron produces 1 as output and its output is only 0 when both inputs are 0. $w_1\big(PL\_N2(PLP)\big) \geq \tau\big(PL\_N2(PLP)\big)$ indicates that the single input neuron $N2$ has the delayer effect in this property, which means if its only input is 1, this neuron will produce 1 in its output. $Inputs = (011)^*(\varepsilon + 0 + 01)$ states that the $Inputs$ list has the oscillation pattern of 011. ε presents an empty string here and $(\varepsilon + 0 + 01)$ shows that $Inputs$ length does not have to be a multiple of 3. This list can end in 0 or 01 and still follows the pattern of 011. Note that in this property, we did not state that $Inputs$ is a binary list because it is implicitly stated by $Inputs = (011)^*(\varepsilon + 0 + 01)$. We want to prove that the output of $N1$ is 1 after time 2, hence $1 < time$. Finally, to ensure that the index is in range in the output array $Output\big(PL\_N1(PLP)\big)[time]$, we need to have $time < length\big(Output\big(PL\_N1(PLP)\big)\big)$. Note that $Output\big(PL\_N1(PLP)\big)$ is a list and $Output\big(PL\_N1(PLP)\big)[time]$ denotes the element at the index $time$ in this list. To provide a better overview of the property, we show a sequence of outputs produced by the two neurons of the positive loop considering the assumptions stated in Property 8 in Table 1. Note that at time 0, both neurons are at the initial state and they have 0 as their output. Starting at time 1, the input list is fed to $N1$, the output of $N1$ is sent as input to $N2$, and the output of $N2$ is transferred to the second input of $N1$.

Table 1: The output sequence of neurons in the positive loop according to assumptions of Property 8

Time	0	1	2	3	4	5	6
$Output(N1)$	0	0	1	1	1	1	...
$Output(N2)$	0	0	0	1	1	1	...
$Inputs$	0	1	1	0	1	1	...

To prove this property, we need to prove a couple of lemmas first. The first lemma states that the output of $N2$ is 1 at the time $time + 1$ whenever the output of $N1$ is 1 at the time $time$. The statement of this lemma is expressed below.

Lemma 3. $\forall \ (Inputs: list \ nat) \ \big(PLP: (PositiveLoop \ Inputs)\big) \ (time: nat),$

$$w_1\big(PL\_N1(PLP)\big) \geq \tau\big(PL\_N1(PLP)\big) \wedge w_2\big(PL\_N1(PLP)\big) \geq \tau\big(PL\_N1(PLP)\big) \wedge$$

$$w_1\big(PL\_N2(PLP)\big) \geq \tau\big(PL\_N2(PLP)\big) \wedge Output\big(PL\_N1(PLP)\big)[time] = 1$$

$$time + 1 < length\Big(Output\big(PL\_N2(PLP)\big)\Big) \rightarrow Output\big(PL\_N2(PLP)\big)[time + 1] = 1$$

The assumptions of this lemma are almost the same assumptions as Property 8. Note that the assumption $Inputs = (011)^*(\varepsilon + 0 + 01)$ is missing here because the output of the neuron $N2$ only directly depends on the output of the neuron $N1$ and only indirectly on $Inputs$. This indirect dependency appears in the `PL_Connection1` and `PL_Connection2` constraints, which refer to $Inputs$. There is a new assumption here, which is $Output\big(PL\_N1(PLP)\big)[time] = 1$. This assumption is the main part of this lemma and expresses that if the output of $N1$ is 1 at the time $time$, the output of $N2$ at the time $time + 1$ is 1. Once again $time + 1 < length\Big(Output\big(PL\_N2(PLP)\big)\Big)$ guarantees the required index constraint in $Output\big(PL\_N2(PLP)\big)[time + 1] = 1$. Note that the output of the length of the $Output(N1)$ and the $Output(N2)$ are always the same and they are always equal to $length(input) + 1$. We omit the proof of $length(Output(N1)) = length(Output(N2)) = length(input) + 1$ and instead give a short explanation. The complete proof is available in the accompanying Coq code as a lemma called `InOutLength`. The proof is a simple induction on the length of the $input$. In the base case, when $Inputs = []$, both neurons hold their initial states and $Output(N1) = Output(N2) = [0]$, which means their length is 1 and the lemma is true for the base case. Assuming that it is true for $length(Inputs) = n$, we can easily prove that for $Inputs' = Inputs + [h]$, and with h as an additional input, we have one more output for both neurons. The proof of Lemma 3 is straightforward and follows directly from the Equations (1) and (2) in Definition 1.

Proof *(of Lemma 3)*. The only input of the neuron $N2$ at the time $time + 1$ is the output of the neuron $N1$ at the time $time$. We write $P1$ and $P2$ to denote the membrane potential function applied to $N1$ and $N2$, respectively. Also, $P1(time)$ represents the membrane potential of $N1$ at the time $time$ and $P2(time)$ represents the membrane potential of $N2$ at the time $time$. Two cases need to be covered here based on Equation (1).

First, we consider that $P2(time) \geq \tau(N2)$ and we prove that $Output(N2)[time + 1] = 1$. According to Equation (1), $P2(time + 1) = w_1(N2) \cdot Output(N1)[time]$. We know that

$Output(N1)[time] = 1$. Therefore, $P2(time + 1) = w_1(N2) \cdot 1 = w_1(N2)$. From the assumption $w_1(PL\_N2(PLP)) = w_1(N2) \geq \tau(PL\_N2(PLP)) = \tau(N2)$, we conclude $P2(time + 1) = w_1(N2) \geq \tau(N2)$. According to Equation (2), since $P2(time + 1) \geq \tau(N2)$, it follows that $Output(N2)[time + 1] = 1$.

Second, we consider that $P2(time) < \tau(N2)$ and we prove that $Output(N2)[time + 1] = 1$. According to Equation (1), $P2(time + 1) = w_1(N2) \cdot Output(N1)[time] + r(N2) \cdot P2(time)$. We know that $Output(N1)[time] = 1$. Therefore, $P2(time + 1) = w_1(N2) \cdot 1 + r(N2) \cdot P2[time]$. Recall that $0 \leq r(N2) \leq 1$ and according to the definition of the positive loop, neuron $N1$ activates $N2$ or $w_1(N2) > 0$. This appears in the definition of the positive loop in Coq shown in Figure 43 as the constraint PL_W3. Because we know that $length(w(N2)) = 1$ by the definition of the positive loop, we can use Lemma 1 introduced in Chapter 5 to conclude from $length(w(N2)) = 1$ and $w_1(N2) > 0$ that $P2(time + 1) \geq 0$ holds. Multiplying two non-negative numbers results in a non-negative number. Thus, $r(N2) \cdot P2(time) \geq 0$, which means $P2(time + 1) = w_1(N2) + r(N2) \cdot P2(time) \geq w_1(N2)$. From this fact and the assumption $w_1(PL\_N2(PLP)) = w_1(N2) \geq \tau(PL\_N2(PLP)) = \tau(N2)$, it follows that $P2(time + 1) \geq w_1(N2) \geq \tau(N2)$. According to Equation (2), $P2(time + 1) \geq \tau(N2)$, which gives us $Output(N2)[time] = 1$.

This completes the proof.

The second lemma states that the output of $N1$ is 1 whenever the input is 1 or the output of $N2$ is 1 at the time before. The statement of this lemma is expressed below.

Lemma 4. $\forall$ $(Inputs: list\ nat)\ (PLP: (PositiveLoop\ Inputs))\ (time: nat)$,

$$w_1(PL\_N1(PLP)) \geq \tau(PL\_N1(PLP)) \wedge w_2(PL\_N1(PLP)) \geq \tau(PL\_N1(PLP)) \wedge$$

$$w_1(PL\_N2(PLP)) \geq \tau(PL\_N2(PLP)) \wedge$$

$$(Inputs[time] = 1 \vee Output(PL\_N2(PLP))[time] = 1) \wedge$$

$$time + 1 < length(Output(PL\_N1(PLP))) \rightarrow Output(PL\_N1(PLP))[time + 1] = 1$$

The assumptions of this lemma are also almost the same assumptions as Property 8. Note that the assumption $Inputs = (011)^*(\varepsilon + 0 + 01)$ is missing here because the output of the neuron $N1$ depends on both the $Inputs$ and the output of the neuron $N2$ at the time $time$, and as stated in the new assumption $\big(Inputs[time] = 1 \vee Output(PL\_N2(PLP))[time] = 1\big)$ when either of them are 1, $Output(N1)$ is 1 at the time $time + 1$. In other words, when one of the inputs of the neuron $N1$ is 1, the value of the other one is not important. Again, we have the assumption $time + 1 < length\big(Output(PL\_N1(PLP))\big)$, which expresses the index constraint. As mentioned before, the length of the output for neuron $N1$ and $N2$ are the same and it is one more than the length of $Inputs$. We just need to be certain that we have enough inputs to produce at least $time + 1$ in the outputs of neuron $N1$, hence we have $time + 1 < length\big(Output(PL\_N1(PLP))\big)$ as an assumption. The proof of this lemma also comes directly from the Equations (1) and (2). To proceed with the proof of Lemma 4, we first need to prove a small lemma, which is very similar to Lemma 1 for a neuron with more than one input.

Lemma 5. $\forall\, (N{:}\, neuron)\ (t,\ n{:}\, nat)\ (l_1, l_2, \ldots, l_t{:}\, list\ nat),$

$$\big(\forall i, 1 \le i \le t, l_i = [x_1^i,\ x_2^i, \ldots, x_n^i] \wedge Bin\_List(l_i)\big) \wedge length\big(w(N)\big) = n \wedge$$

$$\big(\forall j, 1 \le j \le n,\ w_j(N) \ge \tau(N)\big) \rightarrow p(N') \ge 0$$

Like Property 6, Lemma 5 is considered for neurons with more than one input. Note that the positive loop contains a neuron with two inputs. Lemma 5 is stated generally for neurons having any number n of inputs. We will use it later for $N1$ of the positive loop with $n = 2$. In the statement of this lemma, the lists $l_1, l_2, \ldots, l_t$ each contain n values for the n inputs at each of the t time steps. In other words, the whole input sequence of the neuron N can be represented as $[l_1, l_2, \ldots, l_t]$ in Coq. Again, we write N' to denote the neuron obtained from initializing N and applying all l_is in the sequence one by one. Thus, $p(N')$ represents the potential value after processing all inputs.

Proof *(of Lemma 5)*. The proof is by induction on t.

Base case: $t = 0$. If there is no input sequence, the neuron keeps its initial status, i.e., $N = N'$. So, $p(N') = p(N) = 0$ because the initial potential value of every neuron is 0. Therefore, $p(N') = 0 \ge 0$.

Induction case: We assume that the property holds for $t - 1$ and shows that it holds for t. We know that $p(N')$ represents the potential value after initializing N and processing $\downarrow_1, \downarrow_2, \ldots, \downarrow_{t-1}$ one by one. We write N'' to denote the neuron obtained from initializing N and applying $\downarrow_1, \downarrow_2, \ldots, \downarrow_{t-1}, \downarrow_t$. In other words, N'' is N' after applying $\downarrow_t$. By the induction hypothesis, we know $p(N') \geq 0$ and we must prove that $p(N'') \geq 0$.

Note that t is the time at which we produced the last output of N''. So, $p(N'')$ corresponds to $p(t)$ and $p(N')$ corresponds to $p(t - 1)$. Again, note that $\tau(N) = \tau(N') = \tau(N'')$ and similar equalities hold for r and w_js for all $1 \leq j \leq n$, so we use them interchangeably.

There are two separate cases here. First, we consider that $p(N') \geq \tau(N)$. Thus, according to Equation (1), $p(N'') = \sum_{j=1}^{n} x_j^t \cdot w_j(N)$. By the assumption $\left(\forall i, 1 \leq i \leq t, \downarrow_i = [x_1^i, x_2^i, \ldots, x_n^i] \wedge Bin\_List(\downarrow_i) \right)$, we know that $\downarrow_t$ is a binary list, which means $x_j^t = 0$ or $x_j^t = 1$. So, $x_j^t \cdot w_j(N) = 0$ or $x_j^t \cdot w_j(N) = w_j(N)$. Also, by the assumption $\left(\forall j, 1 \leq j \leq n, \ w_j(N) \geq \tau(N) \right)$, we can conclude that $w_j(N) \geq \tau(N) > 0$. Thus, we can conclude that $x_j^t \cdot w_j(N) \geq 0$. Therefore, if we sum $x_j^t \cdot w_j(N)$ for all $1 \leq j \leq n$ and both sides of the inequality $x_j^t \cdot w_j(N) \geq 0$, we will have $p(N'') = \sum_{j=1}^{n} x_j^t \cdot w_j(N) \geq 0$.

Second, we consider the case that $p(N') < \tau(N)$. Thus, according to Equation (1), $p(N'') = \sum_{j=1}^{n} x_j^t \cdot w_j(N) + r(N) \cdot p(N')$. Using the same reasoning, we can conclude that $\sum_{j=1}^{n} x_j^t \cdot w_j(N) \geq 0$. By the induction hypothesis, we know that $p(N') \geq 0$. Also, we know that the leak factor is between 0 and 1, namely $0 \leq r(N) \leq 1$, which means $r(N)$ is non-negative. Knowing that $p(N') \geq 0$ and $r(N) \geq 0$, we can conclude that $r(N) \cdot p(N') \geq 0$. Therefore, by adding both sides of the inequalities $\sum_{j=1}^{n} x_j^t \cdot w_j(N) \geq 0$ and $r(N) \cdot p(N') \geq 0$, we have $p(N'') = \sum_{j=1}^{n} x_j^t \cdot w_j(N) + r(N) \cdot p(N') \geq 0$.

This completes the proof. Thus, we showed that it is always the case that the potential value of a neuron with input weights all greater than or equal to its activation threshold is non-negative. Now, we are ready to present the proof of Lemma 4.

Proof *(of Lemma 4)*. The inputs of the neuron $N1$ at the time $time + 1$ are $Inputs[time]$ and $Output(N2)[time]$. Similar to the proof of Lemma 3, we write $P1$ and $P2$ to denote the membrane potential function applied to $N1$ and $N2$, respectively. Also, $P1(time)$ represents the membrane potential of $N1$ at the time $time$ and $P2(time)$ represents the membrane potential of $N2$ at the time $time$. Two cases need to be covered here based on Equation (1).

First, we consider that $P1(time) \geq \tau(N1)$ and we prove that $Output(N1)[time + 1] = 1$. According to Equation (1), $P1(time + 1) = w_1(N1) \cdot Inputs[time] + w_2(N1) \cdot Output(N2)[time]$. We know that $Inputs[time] = 1 \vee Output(N2)[time] = 1$. Based on this assumption, there are three possibilities which are:

$$P1(time + 1) = w_1(N1) \cdot 1 + w_2(N1) \cdot 0 = w_1(N1) \text{ or}$$

$$P1(time + 1) = w_1(N1) \cdot 0 + w_2(N1) \cdot 1 = w_2(N1) \text{ or}$$

$$P1(time + 1) = w_1(N1) \cdot 1 + w_2(N1) \cdot 1 = w_1(N1) + w_2(N1)$$

From the assumptions $w_1\big(PL\_N1(PLP)\big) = w_1(N1) \geq \tau(PL\_N1) = \tau(N1)$ and $w_2\big(PLP(PL\_N1)\big) = w_2(N1) \geq \tau(PL\_N1) = \tau(N1)$, we can conclude that $P1(time + 1) = w_1(N1) \geq \tau(N1)$, $P1(time + 1) = w_2(N1) \geq \tau(N1)$, and $P1(time + 1) = w_1(N1) + w_2(N1) \geq 2\tau(N1) \geq \tau(N1)$ for the three cases above respectively. In all cases $P1(time + 1) \geq \tau(N1)$ and according to Equation (2), from $P1(time + 1) \geq \tau(N1)$, we can conclude that $Output(N1)[time + 1] = 1$.

Second, we consider the case that $P1(time) < \tau(N1)$ and we prove that $Output(N1)[time + 1] = 1$. According to Equation (1), $P1(time + 1) = w_1(N1) \cdot Inputs[time] + w_2(N1) \cdot Output(N2)[time] + r(N1) \cdot P1(time)$. We know that $Inputs[time] = 1 \vee Output(N2)[time] = 1$. Based on this assumption, there are three possibilities which are:

$$P1(time + 1) = w_1(N1) \cdot 1 + w_2(N1) \cdot 0 + r(N1) \cdot P1(time)$$

$$= w_1(N1) + r(N1) \cdot P1(time) \text{ or}$$

$$P1(time + 1) = w_1(N1) \cdot 0 + w_2(N1) \cdot 1 + r(N1) \cdot P1(time)$$

$$= w_2(N1) + r(N1) \cdot P1(time) \text{ or}$$

$$P1(time + 1) = w_1(N1) \cdot 1 + w_2(N1) \cdot 1 + r(N1) \cdot P1(time)$$

$$= w_1(N1) + w_2(N1) + r(N1) \cdot P1(time)$$

Recall that $0 \le r(N2) \le 1$ and similarly, based on the assumptions $w_1\big(PL\_N1(PLP)\big) = w_1(N1) \ge \tau(PL\_N1) = \tau(N1)$ and $w_2\big(PL\_N1(PLP)\big) = w_2(N1) \ge \tau(PL\_N1) = \tau(N1)$, both input weights of neuron $N1$ are greater than or equal to the threshold of $N1$. This means we can use Lemma 5 and conclude that $P1(time) \ge 0$. Multiplying two non-negative numbers results in a non-negative number. Thus, $r(N1) \cdot P1(time) \ge 0$, which means $P1(time + 1) = w_1(N1) + r(N1) \cdot P1(time) \ge \tau(N1)$, $\quad P1(time + 1) = w_2(N1) + r(N1) \cdot P1(time) \ge \tau(N1)$, $\quad$ and $P1(time + 1) = w_1(N1) + w_2(N1) + r(N1) \cdot P1(time) \ge 2\tau(N1) \ge \tau(N1)$ for the three cases above respectively. $P1(time + 1)$ has the same value as the previous case for these three cases plus a non-negative value which means the inequality $P1(time + 1) \ge \tau(N1)$ holds. According to Equation (2), when $P1(time + 1) \ge \tau(N1)$, we can conclude that $Output(N1)[time + 1] = 1$.

This completes the proof.

Now, we are ready to prove Property 8.

Proof *(of Property 8)*. To prove Property 8, we need to use Lemma 3 and Lemma 4. The first three assumptions of Property 8 and Lemma 4 are the same. Basically, Lemma 4 states that by having the first three assumptions of Property 8, if either inputs of neuron $N1$ are 1 at the time $time$, which is stated by the assumption $\big(Inputs[time] = 1 \vee Output(PL\_N2(PLP))[time] = 1\big)$, then $Output(N1)$ is 1 at the time $time + 1$, which is stated by $Output\big(PL\_N1(PLP)\big)[time + 1] = 1$. Note that $time$ is universally quantified in the statement of Lemma 4 and can be instantiated by any natural number. We instantiate it by $time - 1$, and based on the assumption $Inputs = (011)^*(\varepsilon + 0 + 01)$ as expressed in Table 1, we know that when $\big((time - 1) \bmod 3\big) = 1$ or $\big((time - 1) \bmod 3\big) = 2$ (the remainder of $time - 1$ divided by 3 is either 1 or 2), then $Inputs[time - 1] = 1$. Note that we have $time < length\big(Output(N1)\big)$ as one of the assumptions of Property 8, which is also needed to apply Lemma 4. Thus, by Lemma 4, we can conclude that for $time > 1$ and $\big[\big((time - 1) \bmod 3\big) = 1$ or $\big((time - 1) \bmod 3\big) = 2\big]$, $Output(N1)[time] = 1$. This means that $Output(N1)[time] = 1$ when $time > 1$ and $[(time \bmod 3) = 2$ or $(time \bmod 3) = 0]$. The only remaining part for the proof is to prove that $Output(N1)[time] = 1$ is also true when $time > 1$ and $(time \bmod 3) = 1$.

At this point, we need to use Lemma 3. Again, the first three assumptions of Property 8 and Lemma 3 are the same. Similarly, Lemma 3 states that by having the first three assumptions of Property 8, if the only input of neuron $N2$ is 1 at the time $time$, which is stated by the assumption $Output(PL\_N1(PLP))[time] = 1$, then $Output(N2)$ is 1 at the time $time + 1$, which is stated by $Output(PL\_N2(PLP))[time + 1] = 1$. Note that $time$ is also universally quantified in the statement of Lemma 3 and can be instantiated by any natural number. We instantiate it by $time - 2$, and by the above reasoning we know that $Output(N1)[time] = 1$ when $time > 1$ and $[(time \bmod 3) = 2$ or $(time \bmod 3) = 0]$. By replacing $time$ with $time - 2$ in this reasoning, we have $Output(N1)[time - 2] = 1$ when $time - 2 > 1$ and $[((time - 2) \bmod 3) = 2$ or $((time - 2) \bmod 3) = 0]$. Thus, by Lemma 3, and considering that $Output(N1)[time - 2] = 1$ when $time - 2 > 1$ and $[((time - 2) \bmod 3) = 2$ or $((time - 2) \bmod 3) = 0]$, we can conclude that $Output(N2)[time - 1] = 1$ when $time - 2 > 1$ and $[((time - 2) \bmod 3) = 2$ or $((time - 2) \bmod 3) = 0]$. Note that we need $time - 1 < length(Output(N1))$ to be true to be able to apply Lemma 3 and because $time < length(Output(N1))$ is among the assumptions of Property 8 and $length(Output(N1)) = length(Output(N2))$, we can conclude that $time - 1 < time < length(Output(N1)) = length(Output(N2))$. This means that $Output(N2)[time - 1] = 1$ when $time > 3$ and $[((time - 1) \bmod 3) = 0$ or $((time - 1) \bmod 3) = 1]$.

We use Lemma 4 again but this time with $Output(N2)[time] = 1$ in the assumption $(Inputs[time] = 1 \vee Output(PL\_N2(PLP))[time] = 1)$. We know that $Output(N2)[time - 1] = 1$ when $time > 3$ and $[((time - 1) \bmod 3) = 0$ or $((time - 1) \bmod 3) = 1]$. By Lemma 4, we can conclude that $Output(N1)[time] = 1$ when $time > 3$ and $[((time - 1) \bmod 3) = 0$ or $((time - 1) \bmod 3) = 1]$. This means that $Output(N1)[time] = 1$ when $time > 3$ and $[(time \bmod 3) = 1$ or $(time \bmod 3) = 2]$. Let us put together the two results we have for $Output(N1)[time]$.

$time > 1$ and $[(time \bmod 3) = 2$ or $(time \bmod 3) = 0] \Rightarrow Output(N1)[time] = 1$.

$time > 3$ and $[(time \bmod 3) = 1$ or $(time \bmod 3) = 2] \Rightarrow Output(N1)[time] = 1$.

We can simplify the assumptions of the second one and just keep the one we need and rewrite these two results as follows:

$time > 1$ and $[(time \bmod 3) = 2 \text{ or } (time \bmod 3) = 0] \Rightarrow Output(N1)[time] = 1$.

$time > 3$ and $(time \bmod 3) = 1 \Rightarrow Output(N1)[time] = 1$.

We know that $time = 2$ implies that $(time \bmod 3) = 2$ and $time = 3$ implies that $(time \bmod 3) = 0$, which mean they are covered by the first case. Therefore, we can mix these two and unify the result as follows:

$time > 1$ implies $Output(N1)[time] = 1$.

This completes the proof.

The next property about the positive loop archetype is a corollary of Property 8. Property 8 is about neuron $N1$. This new property states that in the positive loop archetype, neuron $N2$ produces spikes only starting at $time = 3$. This property is stated as follows:

Property 9. $\forall$ (*Inputs*: *list nat*) (*PLP*: (*PositiveLoop Inputs*)) (*time*: *nat*),

$$w_1\big(PL\_N1(PLP)\big) \geq \tau\big(PL\_N1(PLP)\big) \wedge w_2\big(PL\_N1(PLP)\big) \geq \tau\big(PL\_N1(PLP)\big) \wedge$$

$$w_1\big(PL\_N2(PLP)\big) \geq \tau\big(PL\_N2(PLP)\big) \wedge Inputs = (011)^*(\varepsilon + 0 + 01) \wedge 2 < time \wedge$$

$$time < length\left(Output\big(PL\_N2(PLP)\big)\right) \rightarrow Output\big(PL\_N2(PLP)\big)[time] = 1$$

Note that in Property 9, almost all assumptions are the same as Property 8 except for $time > 2$ and $time < Output\big(PL\_N2(PLP)\big)$. The former one expresses that neuron $N2$ starts emitting spikes with a delay of 1 in comparison to neuron $N1$. The latter one ensures that we have enough output produced similar to Property 8 but here for $N2$ instead of $N1$.

Proof *(of Property 9)*. We know that since $time > 2$ it is also the case that $time > 1$. Also, because $Output(N1)$ has the same length as $Output(N2)$, and $time < Output\big(PL\_N2(PLP)\big)$, it follows that $time < Output\big(PL\_N1(PLP)\big)$. This means we can use Property 8 and conclude that for $time > 1$, $Output(N1)[time] = 1$. Now, since we have the first three assumptions of Lemma 3 because they are the same as the first three assumptions of this property, if we instantiate *time* in the statement of Lemma 3 with $time - 1$, we can conclude that $Output(N2)[time] = 1$ when $time - 1 > 1$ and $Output(N1)[time - 1] = 1$, which means when $time > 2$, $Output(N2)[time] = 1$.

This completes the proof.

The statement of Property 8 in Coq is shown in Figure 45. Recall that `A /\ B /\ C -> R` is the logical equivalent of `A -> B -> C -> R`. The first three assumptions in the statement of `TwoPositiveLoopAmplifier1` represent $w_1(PL\_N1(PLP)) \geq \tau(PL\_N1(PLP))$, $w_2(PL\_N1(PLP)) \geq \tau(PL\_N1(PLP))$, and $w_1(PL\_N2(PLP)) \geq \tau(PL\_N2(PLP))$ respectively. `Pattern` is a function that takes two lists and a natural number as inputs and checks if the first list follows the pattern given in the second list starting from the given natural number. For example, the list `[1;1;0;1;1;1;0;1;1;1;0]` follows the pattern in the list `[1;1;0;1]` starting at index 0. The function `rev` is from the Coq library; it takes a list as input and returns a list L is a list containing elements of L in the reverse order. Recall that for making induction in the proofs easier, we keep the input list backward. Thus, `(rev Inputs)` should follow the pattern `[0;1;1]` starting at index 0. In other words, `Pattern (rev Inputs) [0%nat;1%nat;1%nat] 0%nat` represents $Inputs = (011)^*(\varepsilon + 0 + 01)$.

```
Theorem TwoPositiveLoopAmplifier1:
  forall (Inputs: list nat) (PLP: @PositiveLoop Inputs) (time: nat),
  Qle_bool (Tau (PL_N1 PLP)) (hd 0 (Weights (PL_N1 PLP)))  = true ->
  (Qle_bool (Tau (PL_N1 PLP)) (hd 0 (tl (Weights (PL_N1 PLP)))))  = true ->
  (Qle_bool (Tau (PL_N2 PLP)) (hd 0 (Weights (PL_N2 PLP))))  = true ->
  Pattern (rev Inputs) [0%nat;1%nat;1%nat] 0%nat ->
  (lt 1%nat time) ->
  (lt time (length (Output (PL_N1 PLP)))) ->
  List.nth time (rev (Output (PL_N1 PLP))) 0%nat = 1%nat.
```

Figure 45. Coq statement of Property 8, the amplifier property for the first neuron in a positive loop

The function `lt` is short for *less than* and is the Coq function for comparing two natural numbers, found in the Coq library of natural numbers. Surely, the notation $<$ is also available in the library of natural numbers for comparing natural numbers, but we use `lt` instead to avoid confusion with $<$ used for rational numbers. Otherwise, importing both natural number and rational libraries causes compile errors. Therefore, `(lt 1%nat time)` expresses $1 < time$ and `(lt time (length (Output (PL_N1 PLP))))` expresses $time <$

$length\big(Output(PL\_N1(PLP))\big)$. `List.nth` is the Coq function that we presented in Figure 17. Recall that this function returns the nth element of a given list. Thus, `List.nth time (rev (Output (PL_N1 PLP))) 0%nat = 1%nat` represents $Output\big(PL\_N1(PLP)\big)[time] = 1$. Once again, we recall that we keep the output list of neurons in the reverse order and that is why we have `(rev (Output (PL_N1 PLP)))` here.

The definition of the function `Pattern`, which is used in the definition of the `TwoPositiveLoopAmplifier1` property, is shown in Figure 46 alongside a helper function `PatternAcc`.

```
Fixpoint nth {T: Type}(l: list T) (ind: nat): option T :=
  match ind with
  | O => match l with
           | nil => None
           | h::t => (Some h)
         end
  | S ind' => match l with
                | nil => None
                | h::t => nth t ind'
              end
end.

Fixpoint PatternAcc {T: Type}(P: list T) (l: list T) (ind: nat): Prop :=
  match P with
  | nil => True
  | h::t => if (beq_nat ind ((length l) - 1)) then
              (nth l ind) = Some h /\ PatternAcc t l 0%nat
            else
              (nth l ind) = Some h /\ PatternAcc t l (ind + 1)
end.

Fixpoint Pattern {T: Type}(P: list T) (l: list T) (ind: nat): Prop :=
  match ind with
  | O => PatternAcc P l 0%nat
  | S ind' => Pattern (tl P) l ind'
end.
```

Figure 46. Definitions of `nth`, `PatternAcc`, and `Pattern` functions in Coq

Like `Pattern`, the function `PatternAcc` is a predicate that takes two lists and a natural. In the definition of both `Pattern` and `PatternAcc`, the first argument is a list called `P`, the second argument is a list called `l`, and the third argument is a natural number called `ind`. The function `nth` that is used in the definition of `PatternAcc` is also shown in Figure 46. This function does the same job as `List.nth` but it returns an `option` instead. In `List.nth`, if there is no nth element in the list, the function just returns the given default value, but in the function `nth`, `None` is returned instead.

Also, if the element at the nth position of the given list is e, the function `List.nth` returns e but the function `nth` returns `(Some e)`. Note that all these functions are polymorphic. The general type T can be instantiated with any type. The role of `ind` in `PatternAcc` is totally different than the role of `ind` in `Pattern`. In the function `Pattern`, `ind` represents the index in P that the pattern, given by `l`, should start from, but in the function `PatternAcc`, this input is used to iterate over elements of `l` starting from the first element of this list. It is reset to the beginning of `l` after finishing a complete occurrence of the give pattern, before starting the next one. The function `Pattern` just skips the first `ind` elements in P and then calls `PatternAcc` to check if the pattern in `l` is followed from the index `ind + 1` in P.

The definition of Property 9 is very similar to the definition of Property 8, as it was in the mathematical definition. This definition is shown in Figure 47. The first four assumptions in the definition of Property 9 are exactly the same as Property 8. `(lt 1%nat time)` expresses $1 <$ *time* and `(lt time (length (Output (PL_N2 PLP))))` expresses *time* $<$ $length\big(Output(PL\_N1(PLP))\big)$. Note that the second neuron in the positive loop starts emitting spikes after time 2 in the amplifier property. In the conclusion of this theorem, `List.nth time (rev (Output (PL_N2 PLP))) 0%nat = 1%nat` represents $Output\big(PL\_N2(PLP)\big)[time] = 1$.

```
Theorem TwoPositiveLoopAmplifier2:
    forall (Inputs: list nat) (PLP: @PositiveLoop Inputs) (time: nat),
    Qle_bool (Tau (PL_N1 PLP)) (hd 0 (Weights (PL_N1 PLP)))  = true ->
    (Qle_bool (Tau (PL_N1 PLP)) (hd 0 (tl (Weights (PL_N1 PLP)))))  = true ->
    (Qle_bool (Tau (PL_N2 PLP)) (hd 0 (Weights (PL_N2 PLP))))  = true ->
    Pattern (rev Inputs) [0%nat;1%nat;1%nat] 0%nat ->
    (lt 2%nat time) ->
    (lt time (length (Output (PL_N2 PLP)))) ->
    List.nth time (rev (Output (PL_N2 PLP))) 0%nat = 1%nat.
```

Figure 47. Coq statement of Property 9, the amplifier property for the second neuron in a positive loop

The statement of Lemma 3 in Coq is shown in Figure 48. This lemma is called `NextTimeN2TPL` in our Coq implementation. As explained in the mathematical definition of this lemma, the first three assumptions are the same as the first three assumptions of Property 8 and Property 9. The assumption `List.nth time (rev (Output (PL_N1 PLP))) 0%nat = 1%nat` represents $Output(PL\_N1(PLP))[time] = 1$. The assumption `(time + 1) <? length (Output (PL_N2 PLP)) = true` expresses $time + 1 < length\big(Output(PL\_N2(PLP))\big)$. The operator `<?` is for comparing natural numbers like `lt` but it returns a `bool` and we have to explicitly state that it is equal to `true`. As for the conclusion of this lemma, `List.nth (time + 1) (rev (Output (PL_N2 PLP))) 0%nat = 1%nat` represents $Output(PL\_N2(PLP))[time + 1] = 1$.

```
Lemma NextOutputN2_TPL:
  forall (Inputs: list nat) (PLP: @PositiveLoop Inputs) (time: nat),
  Qle_bool (Tau (PL_N1 PLP)) (hd 0 (Weights (PL_N1 PLP)))  = true ->
  (Qle_bool (Tau (PL_N1 PLP)) (hd 0 (tl (Weights (PL_N1 PLP)))))  = true ->
  (Qle_bool (Tau (PL_N2 PLP)) (hd 0 (Weights (PL_N2 PLP))))  = true ->
  (hd 0%nat (tl (Output (PL_N1 PLP))) = 1%nat) ->
   hd 0%nat (Output (PL_N2 PLP)) = 1%nat.

Lemma NextTimeN2TPL:
  forall (Inputs: list nat) (PLP: @PositiveLoop Inputs) (time: nat),
  Qle_bool (Tau (PL_N1 PLP)) (hd 0 (Weights (PL_N1 PLP)))  = true ->
  (Qle_bool (Tau (PL_N1 PLP)) (hd 0 (tl (Weights (PL_N1 PLP)))))  = true ->
  (Qle_bool (Tau (PL_N2 PLP)) (hd 0 (Weights (PL_N2 PLP))))  = true ->
  List.nth time (rev (Output (PL_N1 PLP))) 0%nat = 1%nat ->
  (time + 1) <? length (Output (PL_N2 PLP)) = true ->
  List.nth (time + 1) (rev (Output (PL_N2 PLP))) 0%nat = 1%nat.
```

Figure 48. Definitions of lemmas `NextOutputN2_TPL` and `NextTimeN2TPL` (Lemma 3) in Coq

Although the mathematical proof of this lemma seems straightforward, the proof in Coq is long and involves proving more lemmas. The lemma `NextTimeN2TPL` needs a helper lemma `NextOutputN2_TPL`, which is also shown in Figure 48. We omitted the mathematical proof of `NextOutputN2_TPL` because not only it is very similar to the proof of `NextTimeN2TPL`, but also `NextTimeN2TPL` is a more general version of `NextOutputN2_TPL`. The lemma `NextOutputN2_TPL` states that if the most recent output of the neuron N1 is 1, then the next output of N2 will be 1. Because we keep the outputs of neurons in the reverse order, the most recent output of the neuron is the head of its output list. In `NextOutputN2_TPL`, because we need the output of N1 at one time unit before the output of N2 is produced, we find it at the head of the tail of (Output N1). It must be equal to 1, which is expressed as (hd 0%nat (tl (Output (PL_N1 PLP))) = 1%nat). Also, the next output of the neuron N2 is at the head of (Output N2). The fact that it must be equal to 1 is expressed in the conclusion of NextOutputN2_TPL as hd 0%nat (Output (PL_N2 PLP)) = 1%nat. In the proof of lemma NextTimeN2TPL, we use the function skipn in Figure 19 to skip to the element time in (Output N1), and then we can use NextOutputN2_TPL to complete the proof.

The statement of Lemma 4 in Coq is shown in Figure 49. This lemma is called NextTimeN1TPL in our Coq implementation. Similar to Lemma 3, the first three assumptions of Lemma 4 are the same as the first three assumptions of Property 8 and Property 9. List.nth time (rev (Inputs)) 0%nat = 1%nat \/ List.nth time (rev (Output (PL_N2 PLP))) 0%nat = 1%nat represents $(Inputs[time] = 1 \lor Output(PL\_N2(PLP))[time] = 1)$. The conclusion of Lemma 4, which is stated as $Output(PL\_N1(PLP))[time + 1] = 1$ in the mathematical definition is represented as List.nth (time + 1) (rev (Output (PL_N1 PLP))) 0%nat = 1%nat in Figure 49.

```
Lemma NextOutputN1_TPL:
  forall (Inputs: list nat) (PLP: @PositiveLoop Inputs) (time: nat),
    Qle_bool (Tau (PL_N1 PLP)) (hd 0 (Weights (PL_N1 PLP)))  = true ->
    (Qle_bool (Tau (PL_N1 PLP)) (hd 0 (tl (Weights (PL_N1 PLP)))))  = true ->
    (Qle_bool (Tau (PL_N2 PLP)) (hd 0 (Weights (PL_N2 PLP))))  = true ->
    (hd 0%nat (Inputs)) = 1%nat \/
    (hd 0%nat (tl (Output (PL_N2 PLP))) = 1%nat) ->
     hd 0%nat (Output (PL_N1 PLP)) = 1%nat.

Lemma NextTimeN1TPL:
  forall (Inputs: list nat) (PLP: @PositiveLoop Inputs) (time: nat),
    Qle_bool (Tau (PL_N1 PLP)) (hd 0 (Weights (PL_N1 PLP)))  = true ->
    (Qle_bool (Tau (PL_N1 PLP)) (hd 0 (tl (Weights (PL_N1 PLP)))))  = true ->
    (Qle_bool (Tau (PL_N2 PLP)) (hd 0 (Weights (PL_N2 PLP))))  = true ->
    List.nth time (rev (Inputs)) 0%nat = 1%nat \/
    List.nth time (rev (Output (PL_N2 PLP))) 0%nat = 1%nat ->
    (time + 1) <? length (Output (PL_N1 PLP)) = true ->
    List.nth (time + 1) (rev (Output (PL_N1 PLP))) 0%nat = 1%nat.
```

Figure 49. Definitions of lemmas NextOutputN1_TPL and NextTimeN1TPL (Lemma 4) in Coq

Similar to Lemma 3, the proof of this lemma needs a helper lemma in Coq. The lemma NextOutputN1_TPL, which is also shown in Figure 49 plays the same role for

NextTimeN1TPL as NextOutputN2_TPL did for NextTimeN2TPL. The first three assumptions of NextOutputN1_TPL are the same as NextTimeN2TPL. The assumption (hd 0%nat (Inputs)) = 1%nat \/ (hd 0%nat (tl (Output (PL_N2 PLP)))) = 1%nat) expresses that either the most recent input or the previous output of neuron N2 are 1 and this implies that the next output of the neuron N1 is 1, which is represented as hd 0%nat (Output (PL_N1 PLP)) = 1%nat. Similarly, in the proof of lemma NextTimeN1TPL, we use the function skipn in Figure 19 to skip to the element time in (Output N2), and then we can use NextOutputN1_TPL to complete the proof.

The assumption $\big(\forall j, 1 \le j \le n\ w_j(N) > \tau(N)\big)$ in the statement of Lemma 5 can be replaced by $\big(\forall j, 1 \le j \le n\ w_j(N) > 0\big)$ while keeping Lemma 5 true. We omit the mathematical proof of this version because it follows the same logic as Lemma 5. In Coq, we proved it as special cases separately for both neurons in the positive loop because we needed their states exactly after applying the input sequence using function AfterNTwoLoopN1 and AfterNTwoLoopN2. These lemmas are called PositiveCurrent1 and PositiveCurrent2 and they are shown in Figure 50.

```
Fixpoint AllPositive (l: list Q): Prop :=
  match l with
  | nil => True
  | h::t => 0 < h /\ AllPositive t
  end.

Lemma InOutLength:
  forall (Inputs: list nat) (PLP: @PositiveLoop Inputs),
  beq_nat (length Inputs + 1%nat) (length (Output (PL_N1 PLP))) = true /\
  beq_nat (length Inputs + 1%nat) (length (Output (PL_N2 PLP))) = true.

Lemma PositiveCurrent1:
  forall (Inputs: list nat) (N M P: Neuron),
  AllPositive (Weights N) ->
  N = AfterNTwoLoopN1 (ResetNeuron M) (ResetNeuron P) Inputs -> 0 <= (Current N).

Lemma PositiveCurrent2:
  forall (Inputs: list nat) (N M P: Neuron),
  AllPositive (Weights N) ->
  N = AfterNTwoLoopN2 (ResetNeuron M) (ResetNeuron P) Inputs -> 0 <= (Current N).
```

Figure 50. Definitions of the function AllPositive and lemmas InOutLength, PositiveCurrent1 and PositiveCurrent2 used in the Coq implementation of Lemma 5

We did not use an instance of the positive loop in their statements because it would complicate their proofs. Instead, we generalize them with neurons of the positive loop in the proofs of Lemma 3 and Lemma 4. The function `AllPositive`, which is also shown in Figure 50, expresses the assumption $\left(\forall j, 1 \leq j \leq n \ w_j(N) > 0\right)$ that all input weights of the neuron N are positive. The lemma `InOutLength`, which was mentioned earlier in the proof of Lemma 3, expresses that the length of the output of the neuron N1 and the neuron N2 are the same and one more than the length of the input sequence is also shown in Figure 50.

The number of neurons in the positive loop is equal to the time delay that the neuron N1 starts emitting spikes. This is not a coincidence. In fact, if we extend the structure to more neurons, the first neuron starts producing 1 in the output at the time equal to the number of neurons. For example, if there are three neurons in the positive loop such that N1 activates N2, and N2 activates N3, and N3 activates N1 with the input sequence fed to N1, then N1 starts producing 1 at time 3, N2 follows N1 at time 4, and N3 follows N2 at time 5. In general, we can say that in a positive loop archetype with n neurons, the first neuron starts producing 1 in its output at time n and the rest of neurons follow with one unit of time delay from the neuron that activates them. The proof of the general version of the positive loop is left as future work.

6.6 The Definition of the Negative Loop Archetype and Two Oscillation Properties

The negative loop archetype is shown in Figure 2(d). As mentioned earlier, this archetype has almost the same structure of the positive loop except that the neuron N2 inhibits the neuron N1 instead of activating it. The neuron N1 still plays an activation role for the neuron N2. Unlike the positive loop, this archetype has a weakening effect over time instead of an amplifying effect. In biology, this archetype can be used to weaken a signal more or less quickly. The definition of this archetype in Coq is shown in Figure 51. The negative loop record is a parameterized record like the positive loop and it takes a list of natural numbers called `Inputs`, which contains the list of inputs to be applied to the neuron N1. Recall that fields of a record in Coq cannot have the same name. That is why we used `NL_N1` and `NL_N2` instead of `PL_N1` and `PL_N2` is the definition of the negative loop. The constraints `NL_NinputN1` and `NL_NinputN2` play the same role for the negative loop as `PL_NinputN1` and `PL_NinputN2` for the positive loop. The constraints about input weights of neurons, namely `NL_PW1` and `NL_PW3` are the same as `PL_PW1` and `PL_PW3` in the positive loop but since the neuron `N1` inhibits the neuron `N2` in the negative loop, `NL_NW2` states that the second input weight of `N1` is negative. Recall that `PL_PW2` states that the second weight of `N1` is positive for the positive loop. Finally, `NL_Connection1` and `NL_Connection2` use the functions `AfterNTwoLoopN1` and `AfterNTwoLoopN2` to apply `Inputs` to the archetype just like `PL_Connection1` and `PL_Connection2`.

```
Record NegativeveLoop {Inputs: list nat} := MakeNegativeLoop
{
  NL_N1: Neuron;
  NL_N2: Neuron;
  NL_NinputN1: (beq_nat (length (Weights PL_N1)) 2%nat) = true;
  NL_NinputN2: (beq_nat (length (Weights PL_N2)) 1%nat) = true;
  NL_PW1: 0 < (hd 0 (Weights NL_N1));
  NL_PW2: (hd 0 (tl (Weights NL_N1))) < 0;
  NL_PW3: 0 < (hd 0 (Weights PL_N2));
  NL_Connection1: Eq_Neuron2 NL_N1 (AfterNTwoLoopN1 (ResetNeuron NL_N1)
                  (ResetNeuron NL_N2) Inputs);
  NL_Connection2: Eq_Neuron2 NL_N2 (AfterNTwoLoopN2 (ResetNeuron NL_N1)
                  (ResetNeuron NL_N2) Inputs)
}.
```

Figure 51. Definition of the negative loop in Coq

Here we introduce an interesting property of the negative loop. The statement of this property is expressed as follows:

Property 10. $\forall$ *(Inputs: list nat) (NLP: (PositiveLoop Inputs)) (time: nat),*

$$w_1\big(NL\_N1(NLP)\big) \geq \tau\big(NL\_N1(NLP)\big) \wedge \big|w_2\big(NL\_N1(NLP)\big)\big| \geq w_1\big(NL\_N1(NLP)\big) \wedge$$

$$w_1\big(NL\_N2(NLP)\big) \geq \tau\big(NL\_N2(NLP)\big) \wedge Inputs = 1^* \rightarrow$$

$$Output\big(NL\_N1(NLP)\big) = 0(1100)^*$$

Similarly, as we did for the positive loop, we use $N1$ to denote $NL\_N1(NLP)$ and $N2$ to denote $NL\_N2(NLP)$. In the statement of this property, $w_1\big(NL\_N1(NLP)\big) \geq \tau\big(NL\_N1(NLP)\big)$ expresses that the first input of the neuron $N1$ can activate this neuron and $w_1\big(NL\_N2(NLP)\big) \geq \tau\big(NL\_N2(NLP)\big)$ expresses that the only input of the neuron $N2$ can activate it. The interesting assumption here is $\big|w_2\big(NL\_N1(NLP)\big)\big| \geq w_1\big(NL\_N1(NLP)\big)$. Note that in the definition of the negative loop $w_2\big(NL\_N1(NLP)\big) < 0$, which causes the inhibition of $N1$ by $N2$. Requiring the absolute value of this weight to be greater than the weight of the other input of $N1$, which is $Inputs$, means that when both inputs of $N1$ are 1, the inhibition effect is more powerful and does not allow $N1$ to produce 1 as its output. Note that whenever both inputs to $N1$ are 1, the weighted sum of the inputs of $N1$ is less than 0, which means that the potential is $1 \cdot w_1(N1) + 1 \cdot w_2(N1) = w_1(N1) + w_2(N1)$ and $w_1(N1) + w_2(N1) < 0 < \tau(N1)$. $Inputs = 1^*$ expresses that the input sequence tries to constantly activate neuron $N1$. In biology, this happens when a neuron receives constant activations from the environment and the negative loop can cool the system down and generate oscillation. Note that here, we also do not need to state that $Inputs$ is a binary list because it is mentioned implicitly by $Inputs = 1^*$. If all these assumptions hold for the negative loop, then the output of $N1$ is an oscillation of the form 1100 starting after the initial output of this neuron, hence we have $Output\big(NL\_N1(NLP)\big) = 0(1100)^*$. A similar conclusion is true for neuron $N2$ with one unit of time delay. In other words, having the same assumptions, we have $Output\big(NL\_N2(NLP)\big) = 00(1100)^*$ as stated in Property 11 as follows:

Property 11. $\forall\ (Inputs: list\ nat)\ (NLP: (PositiveLoop\ Inputs))\ (time: nat),$

$$w_1\big(NL\_N1(NLP)\big) \geq \tau\big(NL\_N1(NLP)\big) \wedge \big|w_2\big(NL\_N1(NLP)\big)\big| \geq w_1\big(NL\_N1(NLP)\big) \wedge$$

$$w_1(NL\_N2(NLP)) \geq \tau(NL\_N2(NLP)) \wedge Inputs = 1^* \rightarrow$$

$$Output\big(NL\_N2(NLP)\big) = 00(1100)^*$$

To provide a better understanding of these properties, we show a sequence of outputs produced by the two neurons of the negative loop considering the assumptions stated in Property 10 and Property 11 in Table 2.

Table 2: The output sequence of neurons in the negative loop based on assumptions of Property 10 and Property 11

Time	0	1	2	3	4	5	6	7	8	9
$Output(N1)$	0	1	1	0	0	1	1	0	0	...
$Output(N2)$	0	0	1	1	0	0	1	1	0	0
$Inputs$	1	1	1	1	1	1	1	1	1	1

Similar to the positive loop at time 0, both neurons are at the initial state and they have 0 as their output. Starting at time 1, the input list is fed to $N1$, the output of $N1$ is sent as input to $N2$, and the output of $N2$ is transferred to the second input of $N1$.

```
Fixpoint All1 (Input: list nat): Prop :=
 match Input with
 | nil => True
 | h::t => (beq_nat h 1%nat) /\ All1 t
 end.

Theorem NegativeLoopN1OutputPattern1100:
  forall (Inputs: list nat) (NLP: @NegativeLoop Inputs) (w1 w2 w3: Q),
  (w1 == (hd 0 (Weights (NL_N1 NLP)))) ->
  (w2 == (hd 0 (tl (Weights (NL_N1 NLP))))) ->
  (w3 == (hd 0 (Weights (NL_N2 NLP)))) ->
  (Qle_bool w1 (Qabs w2)) = true ->
  (Qle_bool (Tau (NL_N1 NLP)) w1) = true ->
  (Qle_bool (Tau (NL_N2 NLP)) w3)  = true ->
  All1 Inputs ->
  Pattern (rev (Output (NL_N1 NLP))) [1%nat;1%nat;0%nat;0%nat] 1%nat.

Theorem NegativeLoopN2OutputPattern1100:
  forall (Inputs: list nat) (NLP: @NegativeLoop Inputs) (w1 w2 w3: Q),
  (w1 == (hd 0 (Weights (NL_N1 NLP)))) ->
  (w2 == (hd 0 (tl (Weights (NL_N1 NLP))))) ->
  (w3 == (hd 0 (Weights (NL_N2 NLP)))) ->
  (Qle_bool w1 (Qabs w2)) = true ->
  (Qle_bool (Tau (NL_N1 NLP)) w1) = true ->
  (Qle_bool (Tau (NL_N2 NLP)) w3)  = true ->
  All1 Inputs ->
  Pattern (rev (Output (NL_N1 NLP))) [1%nat;1%nat;0%nat;0%nat] 2%nat.
```

Figure 52. Statement of the function All1 and the oscillation of 1100 properties (Properties 8 and 9) for a negative loop

The statements of Property 10 and Property 11 in Coq are shown in Figure 52. These properties in Coq are called NegativeLoopN1OutputPattern1100 and NegativeLoopN2OutputPattern1100 respectively. Assumptions (w1 == (hd 0 (Weights (NL_N1 NLP)))), (w2 == (hd 0 (tl (Weights (NL_N1 NLP))))), and (w3 == (hd 0 (Weights (NL_N2 NLP)))) are just for facilitating the definitions of these properties. They give a name to the weights of neurons. The assumption (Qle_bool w1 (Qabs w2) = true expresses $|w_2(NL\_N1(NLP))| \geq w_1(NL\_N1(NLP))$. The function Qabs is a built-in function in the library of rational numbers in Coq that takes a rational number and return its absolute value. The assumptions `(Qle_bool (Tau (NL_N1 NLP)) w1) = true` and `(Qle_bool (Tau (NL_N2 NLP)) w3) = true` represent $w_1(NL\_N1(NLP)) \geq \tau(NL\_N1(NLP))$ and $w_1(NL\_N2(NLP)) \geq \tau(NL\_N2(NLP))$, respectively, in the mathematical definitions of these properties.

Finally, the function `All1` that is applied to `Inputs` and is also shown in Figure 52 expresses that all elements in `Inputs` are 1, or as stated mathematically, $Inputs = 1^*$. As for the conclusions, we use the function `Pattern`, which was introduced earlier in Figure 46, to express that the output of `N1` follows the pattern 1100 starting at index 1 in Property 10 and the output of `N2` follows the same pattern at index 2 in Property 11. Once again, recall that we keep the list of the output of the neurons in the reverse order, hence we need to use the function `rev` from the Coq list library. Mathematical proofs of these two properties and their verifications in Coq are left as future work.

6.7 The Definition of the Contralateral Inhibition Archetype and the Winner Takes All Properties

The last archetype that we discuss in this book is the *Contralateral Inhibition*, which is shown in Figure 2(f). As can be seen in Figure 2(f), this archetype also has two neurons but both of these neurons have two inputs. There are two input sequences to the contralateral inhibition. The first one is fed to the first neuron and the second one is fed to the second neuron. The other input of each neuron comes from the output of the other neuron. Each neuron plays an inhibition role for the other neuron.

Note that the weight of the second input of each neuron, which is connected to the output of the other neuron is negative as shown by a filled black circle in Figure 2(f. Thus, each neuron inhibits the other one. The definition of this archetype in Coq is shown in Figure 53. Once again, we need new names for the fields of this record, hence `CI_N1` and `CI_N2` represent the neurons `N1` and `N2` in this archetype. The constraints `CI_NinputN1` and `CI_NinputN2` state than both neurons have two inputs. We have two inputs for this archetype, which are `Input1` and `Input2` and the constraint `InputLengthEq` states that they have the same number of elements. The constraints `CI_PW1` and `CI_PW3` express that the weights of the first input of each neuron, which come from

`Input1` for `N1` and `Input2` for `N2`, are positive. On the other hand, `CI_PW2` and `CI_PW4` express the inhibitions that are applied to the other input of each neuron via the output of the other neuron, by stating that the second input weight of each neuron is negative.

```
Record ContralateralInhibition {Input1 Input2: list nat} :=
                        MakeContralateralInhibition
{
  CI_N1: Neuron;
  CI_N2: Neuron;
  CI_NinputN1: (beq_nat (length (Weights CI_N1)) 2%nat) = true;
  CI_NinputN2: (beq_nat (length (Weights CI_N2)) 2%nat) = true;
  InputLengthEq: (length Input1) = (length Input2);
  CI_PW1: 0 < (hd 0 (Weights CI_N1));
  CI_PW2: (hd 0 (tl (Weights CI_N1))) < 0;
  CI_PW3: 0 < (hd 0 (Weights CI_N2));
  CI_PW4: (hd 0 (tl (Weights CI_N2))) < 0;
  CI_Connection1:
  Eq_Neuron2 CI_N1 (AfterNCIN1
                    (ResetNeuron CI_N1) (ResetNeuron CI_N2) Input1 Input2);
  CI_Connection2:
  Eq_Neuron2 CI_N2 (AfterNCIN2
                    (ResetNeuron CI_N1) (ResetNeuron CI_N2) Input1 Input2)
}.
```

Figure 53. The definition of the contralateral inhibition archetype in Coq

The structure of the contralateral inhibition is different from the positive and the negative loop. Thus, we need new functions to express how the input sequences are applied. The functions `AfterNCIN1` and `AfterNCIN2`, which are shown in Figure 54 take both neurons and both input sequences as arguments and apply the input elements one by one according to the structure of the contralateral inhibition. The only difference is `AfterNCIN1` returns the neuron `N1` after applying all elements in the input sequences but `AfterNCIN2` returns the neuron `N2` after processing its inputs. These functions need not be mutually recursive and they are written as two separate regular recursive functions. Note that in each recursive call of `AfterNCIN1` and `AfterNCIN2`, two input lists of two elements are created to be used as the inputs in the application of the `NextNeuron` function, which was defined in Figure 26. In the function `AfterNCIN1`, the list of two inputs of `N1` is `[h; (hd (2%nat) (Output N2))]`, which includes the first element of the input in `Inp1` and the most recent output of `N2`. Similarly, the list of two inputs of `N2` is `[(hd (0%nat) Inp2); (hd (2%nat) (Output N1))]`, which includes the first element of the input in `Inp2` and the most recent output of `N1`. Note that the pattern matching is on `Inp1` in `AfterNCIN1` but it is on `Inp2` in `AfterNCIN2`. That is why in the function `AfterNCIN2`, the list of two inputs of N1 is `[(hd (0%nat) Inp1);(hd (2%nat) (Output N2))]`, and the list of two inputs of N2 is `[h;(hd (2%nat) (Output N1))]`.

```
Fixpoint AfterNCIN1 (N1 N2: Neuron) (Inp1 Inp2:list nat): Neuron :=
  match Inp1 with
  | nil => N1
  | h::t => AfterNCIN1
              (NextNeuron N1 [h;(hd (2%nat) (Output N2))])
              (NextNeuron N2 [(hd (0%nat) Inp2);(hd (2%nat) (Output N1))])
              t (tl Inp2)
  end.

Fixpoint AfterNCIN2 (N1 N2: Neuron) (Inp1 Inp2:list nat): Neuron :=
  match Inp2 with
  | nil => N2
  | h::t => AfterNCIN2
              (NextNeuron N1 [(hd (0%nat) Inp1);(hd (2%nat) (Output N2))])
              (NextNeuron N2 [h;(hd (2%nat) (Output N1))])
              (tl Inp1) t
  end.
```

Figure 54. The definition of functions `AfterNCIN1` and `AfterNCIN2` in Coq

The contralateral inhibition is known for being able to generate a behavior of the kind *winner takes all* when one neuron (the winner) is constantly activated and the other neuron (the loser) is constantly inhibited. This behavior is the focus of the next property, which expresses the contralateral inhibition is able to make a neuron produce 1 in its output while the other neuron produces only 0. We express these two effects in two properties as stated as follows:

Property 12. $\forall$ (*Input1, Input2: list nat*) (*CLI*: (*ContralateralInhibition Input1 Input2*)),

$$w_1\big(CI\_N1(CLI)\big) \geq \tau\big(C\!\downarrow\!\_N1(CLI)\big) \wedge \big|w_2\big(CI\_N1(CLI)\big)\big| \geq w_1\big(CI\_N1(CLI)\big) \wedge$$

$$w_1\big(CI\_N2(CLI)\big) \geq \tau\big(C\!\downarrow\!\_N2(CLI)\big) \wedge w_1\big(CI\_N2(CLI)\big) \geq \big|w_2\big(CI\_N2(CLI)\big)\big| \wedge$$

$$Input1 = 1^* \wedge Input2 = 1^* \rightarrow Output\big(C\!\downarrow\!\_N2(CLI)\big) = 01^*$$

Property 13. $\forall$ (*Input1, Input2: list nat*) (*CLI*: (*ContralateralInhibition Input1 Input2*)),

$$w_1\big(CI\_N1(CLI)\big) \geq \tau\big(C\!\downarrow\!\_N1(CLI)\big) \wedge \big|w_2\big(CI\_N1(CLI)\big)\big| \geq w_1\big(CI\_N1(CLI)\big) \wedge$$

$$w_1\big(CI\_N2(CLI)\big) \geq \tau\big(C\!\downarrow\!\_N2(CLI)\big) \wedge w_1\big(CI\_N2(CLI)\big) \geq \big|w_2\big(CI\_N2(CLI)\big)\big| \wedge$$

$$Input1 = 1^* \land Input2 = 1^* \rightarrow Output\big(C{\downarrow}\_N1(CLI)\big) = 0(0+1)0^*$$

In the statement of these properties, the assumption $w_1\big(CI\_N1(CLI)\big) \geq \tau\big(C{\downarrow}\_N1(CLI)\big)$ implies that when the current input in $Input1$ is 1 and the other input of neuron $N1$ coming from the output of neuron $N2$ is 0, the neuron $N1$ produces 1 as the output. This is because the first input weight is greater than or equal to the threshold of $N1$. The assumption $w_1\big(CI\_N2(CLI)\big) \geq \tau\big(C{\downarrow}\_N2(CLI)\big)$ implies the same for neuron $N2$. The interesting assumptions in these properties are two assumptions that play opposite roles for $N1$ and $N2$. The assumption $\big|w_2\big(CI\_N1(CLI)\big)\big| \geq w_1\big(CI\_N1(CLI)\big)$ states that the second input of N1 that comes from the output of $N2$ and inhibits $N1$ has a stronger weight than the first input of $N1$ which comes from $Input1$ and plays the activation role. This means that if both inputs of $N1$ are 1, this neuron cannot produce 1 in its output. On the other hand, $w_1\big(CI\_N2(CLI)\big) \geq \big|w_2\big(CI\_N2(CLI)\big)\big|$ states the opposite, which means the first input of $N2$ which comes from $Input2$ and activates $N2$, is stronger than the second input of $N2$ which comes from the output of $N1$ and inhibits $N2$. This means that if both inputs of $N2$ are 1, this neuron produces 1 in its output. The assumptions $Input1 = 1^*$ and $Input2 = 1^*$ express that both $Input1$ and $Input2$ include only 1s. The conclusion of Property 12, namely $Output\big(CI\_N2(CLI)\big) = 01^*$ states that the neuron $N2$ only produces 1 starting time 1. As for the conclusion of Property 13, $Output\big(CI\_N1(CLI)\big) = 0(0+1)0^*$ expresses that the neuron $N1$ starts producing 0 after time 2. In other words, $N1$ is inhibited and $N2$ is activated after time 2 in the contralateral inhibition archetype.

Table 3: The output sequence of neurons in the contralateral inhibition archetype according to assumptions of Properties 12 and 13

Time	0	1	2	3	4	5	6	7	8	9
$Output(N1)$	0	1	0	0	0	0	0	0	0	...
$Output(N2)$	0	1	1	1	1	1	1	1	1	...
$Input1$	1	1	1	1	1	1	1	1	1	...
$Input2$	1	1	1	1	1	1	1	1	1	...

To provide a better understanding of these properties, we show a sequence of outputs produced by the two neurons of the contralateral inhibition considering the assumptions stated in Property 12 and Property 13 in Table 2. Both neurons start at the initial state with 0 as their output. Starting at time 1, the input list *Input*1 is fed to *N*1, the output of *N*1 is sent as the second input of *N*2, the input list *Input*2 is fed to *N*2 and the output of *N*2 is sent as the second input of *N*1.

```coq
Fixpoint All0 (Input: list nat): Prop :=
  match Input with
  | nil => True
  | h::t => (beq_nat h 0%nat) /\ All1 t
  end.

Theorem CIN2All1:
  forall (Input1 Input2: list nat)
         (CLI: @ContralateralInhibition Input1 Input2) (w1 w2 w3 w4: Q),
         w1 == (hd 0 (Weights (CI_N1 CLI))) ->
         w2 == (hd 0 (tl (Weights (CI_N1 CLI)))) ->
         w3 == (hd 0 (Weights (CI_N2 CLI))) ->
         w4 == (hd 0 (tl (Weights (CI_N2 CLI)))) ->
         (Qle_bool (Tau (CI_N1 CLI)) w1) = true ->
         (Qle_bool w1 (Qabs w2)) = true ->
         (Qle_bool (Tau (CI_N2 CLI)) w3) = true ->
         (Qle_bool (Qabs w4) w3) = true ->
         All1 Input1 ->
         All1 Input2 -> (All1 (tl (rev (Output (CI_N2 CLI))))).

Theorem CIN1All0:
  forall (Input1 Input2: list nat)
         (CLI: @ContralateralInhibition Input1 Input2) (w1 w2 w3 w4: Q),
         w1 == (hd 0 (Weights (CI_N1 CLI))) ->
         w2 == (hd 0 (tl (Weights (CI_N1 CLI)))) ->
         w3 == (hd 0 (Weights (CI_N2 CLI))) ->
         w4 == (hd 0 (tl (Weights (CI_N2 CLI)))) ->
         (Qle_bool (Tau (CI_N1 CLI)) w1) = true ->
         (Qle_bool w1 (Qabs w2)) = true ->
         (Qle_bool (Tau (CI_N2 CLI)) w3) = true ->
         (Qle_bool (Qabs w4) w3) = true ->
         All1 Input1 ->
         All1 Input2 -> (All0 (tl (tl (rev (Output (CI_N2 CLI)))))).
```

Figure 55. Statement of the function `All0` and properties `CIN2All1` and `CIN1All0` (Properties 10 and 11) for a contralateral inhibition

The statement of Property 12 and Property 13 in Coq are shown in Figure 55. These properties are called `CIN2All1` and `CIN1All0` in Coq. Similar to properties in Figure 52 about the negative loop, the first four assumptions of these properties are there to give names to $w1$, $w2$, $w3$, and $w4$

to `(hd 0 (Weights (CI_N1 CLI)))`, `(hd 0 (tl (Weights (CI_N1 CLI))))`, `(hd 0 (Weights (CI_N2 CLI)))`, and `(hd 0 (tl (Weights (CI_N2 CLI))))`, respectively.

The assumption `(Qle_bool (Tau (CI_N1 CLI)) w1) = true` expresses $w_1\big(CI\_N1(CLI)\big) \geq \tau\big(C{\downarrow}\_N1(CLI)\big)$, the assumption `(Qle_bool w1 (Qabs w2)) = true` expresses $\big|w_2\big(CI\_N1(CLI)\big)\big| \geq w_1\big(CI\_N1(CL{\downarrow})\big)$, the assumption `(Qle_bool (Tau (CI_N2 CLI)) w3) = true` expresses $w_1\big(CI\_N2(CLI)\big) \geq \tau\big(C{\downarrow}\_N2(CLI)\big)$, and finally the assumption `(Qle_bool (Qabs w4) w3) = true` expresses $w_1\big(CI\_N2(CLI)\big) \geq \big|w_2\big(CI\_N2(CLI)\big)\big|$. The assumptions `All1 Input1` and `All1 Input2` use the function `All1` in Figure 52 to express that all elements of both input sequence `Input1` and `Input2` must be 1. In the conclusion of `CIN2All1`, which is `(All1 (tl (rev (Output (CI_N2 CLI)))))`, we use the functions `All1` and `tl` to express that every output in the output of the neuron N2 is 1 excluding the head of this list, which means all elements of this list starting at time 1. As for the conclusion of `CIN1All0`, to express that the output of N1 is 0 starting time 2, we need the function `tl` twice as stated in `(All0 (tl (tl (rev (Output (CI_N2 CLI))))))`. The function `All0`, which is also shown in Figure 55, is very similar to `All1` and is used in the statement of the result of `CIN1All0`. Both mathematical proofs and verifications of these properties are left as future work.

Chapter 7

Composition of Archetypes and Their Properties

In this chapter, we explain how two archetypes can be coupled together. As mentioned earlier, archetypes are associated with small functions for doing simple tasks such as delaying, filtering, amplifying, etc. Composition of archetypes gives us more complicated functions such as rhythmic motions in the human body like walking, breathing, running, etc. There are two major types of compositions of archetypes in the literature [20, 26, 27], which are the series and the nested compositions. In this chapter, first we introduce these two types of compositions of archetypes. Then, as an example, we take a series of delayer neurons and a positive loop and couple them together to make a new functional structure. Finally, we introduce and prove a property about this composition and introduce some possible other compositions.

7.1 The Series Composition

In this type of coupling, the internal structure of archetypes does not have any effect on their composition. In other words, we can consider archetypes as a black box and we can connect the output of one archetype to the input of another archetype. Surely, an archetype can have more than one input, such as contralateral inhibition, and since there are two or more neurons in an archetype, the output of more than one neuron can be considered as the output of the composition. Here, we consider only cases where there is one input and one output of the archetypes involved in the composition.

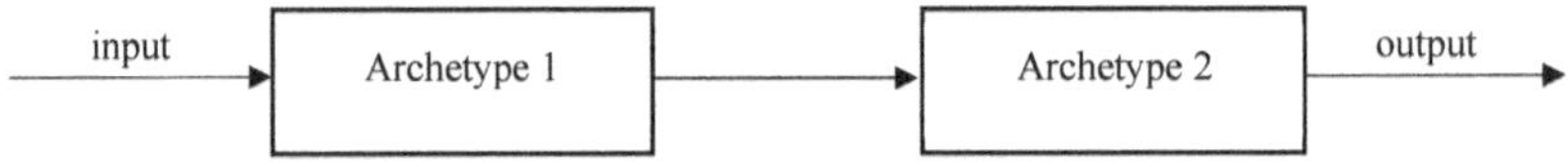

Figure 56. Two archetypes in a Series composition

For the series composition, as shown in Figure 56, we just connect the output of the first archetype to the input of the second archetype to couple them. In this composition, the input of Archetype 1 is the input of the series composition and the output of Archetype 2 is the output of the series composition. The output of Archetype 1 is fed as the input to Archetype 2. As can be seen, in this composition, archetypes are just black boxes and we need not know what structure they have inside. In other words, we can replace these archetypes by different archetypes to create different compositions. In Section 7.3, we show an example of this type of coupling using two archetypes that we introduced in Chapter 6. The series composition with more inputs and outputs is similar except that it may have several connections between outputs of the first archetype and inputs of the second archetype, which can create different outcomes. Also, all or some inputs of the first archetype can be considered as the inputs of the series composition, and all or some outputs of the second archetype can be considered as the outputs of the series composition. The series composition can be extended easily by connecting more archetypes or two or more series compositions together. These diverse couplings can be used to create different functionalities in the human neural network. In this book, we consider only the properties of the simple coupling shown in Figure 56, and leave more complicated structures for future work. Some series compositions are discussed and verified by model checkers in [20, 27].

7.2 The Nested Composition

The second type of composition that we introduce in this book, is the nested composition. In this type of coupling one of the archetypes is nested inside the other one. Like the series composition, archetypes with more inputs or more outputs can be used to create different functionalities. Also, this kind of composition can create a diverse functionality based on the position of the nested archetype in the outer archetype. Unlike the series composition, we cannot consider every archetype as a black box because for the outer archetype, we need to know its structure in order to place the nested archetype inside it.

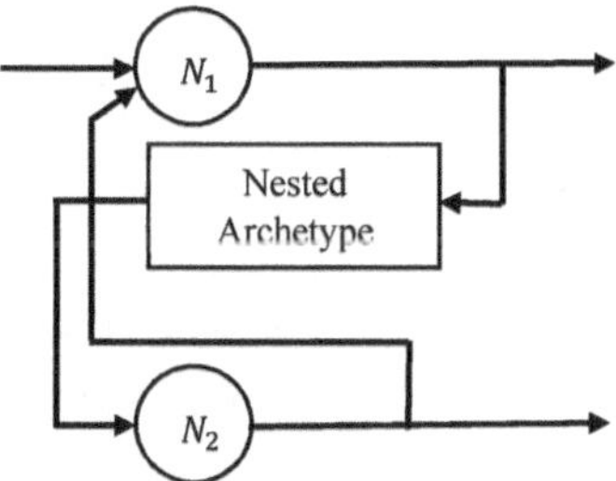

Figure 57. Nested composition of an archetype in the positive loop

As an example, a nested composition is shown in Figure 57 using the structure of the positive loop as the outer archetype. In this composition, the output of the first neuron of the positive loop is fed as the input of the nested archetype and the output of this archetype plays the role of the input of the second neuron in the structure of the positive loop. As can be seen, we cannot just see the outer archetype as a black box. For example, in Figure 57, we need to know what the structure of the outer archetype is and where to place the nested archetype to achieve the desired functionality. Needless to say, placing the nested archetype between the output of $N2$ and the second input of $N1$ can create a totally different nested composition. On the other hand, the nested archetype can still be seen as a black box and we can replace it with any archetype. We do not discuss properties of this type of coupling in this book. Some nested compositions are discussed and verified by model checkers in [20, 27].

7.3 Composition of the Series of Single-Input Neurons and the Positive Loop

In this section, we present a series composition of a positive loop and a series of single-input neurons. Then, we introduce and prove two properties about this coupling. As mentioned earlier, by replacing Archetype 1 and Archetype 2 in Figure 56, we obtain this series composition. Here, we replace the first archetype by a series of single-input neurons and the second archetype by a positive loop. Both archetypes were introduced in Chapter 6. The result is shown in Figure 58.

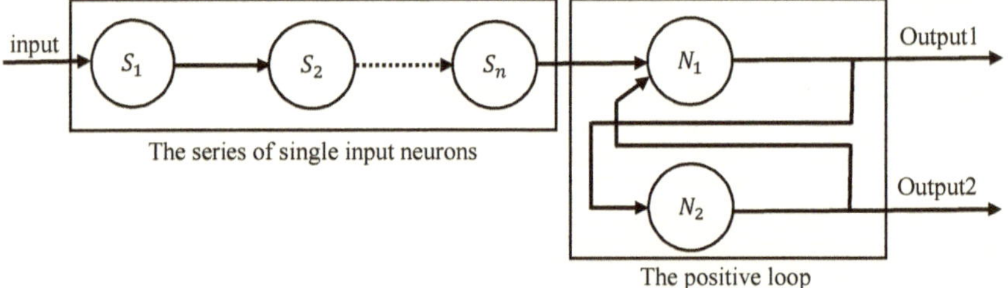

Figure 58. A series composition of a series of single input neurons and a positive loop

In Figure 58, the input of the composition is the input of the series of single input neurons. We consider both outputs for this composition. The first output of the composition is the output of the neuron $N1$ in the positive loop and the second output of this coupling is the output of the neuron $N2$ in the positive loop. The output of the series composition is fed to the positive loop as the first input of the neuron N1. Recall that if all neurons in the series of single input neurons are delayers, this archetype transfers the input signal with a delay of n zeros, where n is the number of single input neurons in the archetype. Also, we know that the positive loop has the ability to produce a persistent sequence of spikes when its input follows the pattern $(011)^*$. Mixing these two properties in the compositions of these archetypes, we can create a delay before producing a persistent sequence of spikes in the output signal. The properties we are going to state in this section are about this composition. The first property is expressed as follows:

Property 14. $\forall$ (*Inputs: list nat*)

$$\big(NSeries: (NeuronSeries\ Inputs)\big)$$

$$\Big(PLP: \big(PositiveLoop\ (NSOutput(NSeries))\big)\Big)\ (time: nat),$$

$$w_1\big(PL\_N1(PLP)\big) \geq \tau\big(PL\_N1(PLP)\big) \wedge w_2\big(PL\_N1(PLP)\big) \geq \tau\big(PL\_N1(PLP)\big) \wedge$$

$$w_1\big(PL\_N2(PLP)\big) \geq \tau(PL\_N2(PLP)) \wedge Inputs = (011)^*(\varepsilon + 0 + 01) \wedge$$

$$length\big(NeuronList(NSeries)\big) = n \wedge n + 1 < time \wedge$$

$$\begin{pmatrix} \forall i\ 0 \leq i < n, & length\big(w(NeuronList(NSeries)[i])\big) = 1 \wedge \\ w_1(NeuronList(NSeries)[i]) > \tau(NeuronList(NSeries)[i]) \end{pmatrix} \wedge$$

$$time < length\Big(Output\big(PL\_N1(PLP)\big)\Big) \rightarrow Output\big(PL\_N1(PLP)\big)[time] = 1$$

The assumptions of this property are a mix of assumptions of Property 7 and Property 8. Namely, the first four assumptions in Property 14 state the same assumptions in Property 8 for the positive loop archetype and they state conditions needed for producing a persistent sequence of spikes starting at a certain time. Like the statement of Property 7, $length\big(NeuronList(NSeries)\big) = n$ states that the number of neurons in the series is n and $\begin{pmatrix} \forall i\ 0 \leq i < n,\ length\big(w(NeuronList(NSeries)[i])\big) = 1 \wedge \\ w_1(NeuronList(NSeries)[i]) > \tau(NeuronList(NSeries)[i]) \end{pmatrix}$ expresses that all neurons in the series are delayers. Note that the output of the series, namely $NSOutput(NSeries)$ is the input of the positive loop because it is the value of the parameter to $PositiveLoop$ in $\Big(PLP: \big(PositiveLoop\ (NSOutput(NSeries))\big)\Big)$. Like the statement of the positive loop, $time <$

$length\left(Output(PL\_N1(PLP))\right)$ ensures that the index is in range. The only assumption here that is different from the assumptions of Property 8 is $n + 1 < time$ instead of $1 < time$. This is because the output of $N1$ has a delay of n zeros before starting to emit spikes. To provide a better understanding of this property, the output sequences of neurons $N1$ and $N2$ are shown in Table 4 according to the assumptions of Property 14.

Table 4: The output sequence of neurons in the composition of a series of delayer neurons and a positive loop according to assumptions of Property 14

Time	0	1	2	...	n	$n+1$	$n+2$	$n+3$	...	$n+k$
$Output(N1)$	0	0	0	...	0	0	1	1	...	1
$Output(N2)$	0	0	0	...	0	0	0	1	...	1
$Output(NSeries)$	0	0	0	0	0	1	1	0	...	1

Note that *Inputs* is not shown in this table but $Inputs = (011)^*(\varepsilon + 0 + 01)$. Using n single input delayer neurons, $Output(NSeries) = 0^n(011)^*(\varepsilon + 0 + 01)$. In other words, *NSeries* creates a delay of n zeros before *Inputs*, and starting at time n, $Output(NSeries)$ follows the pattern $(011)^*(\varepsilon + 0 + 01)$. As can be seen, $N1$ starts producing 1 in its output at time $n + 2$ with n more delays in comparison to the positive loop, and given by the series of n delayers. Similarly, $N2$ starts producing 1 in its output at time $n + 3$ with n more delays in comparison to the positive loop. The proof of this property is straightforward and it follows the same reasoning as Property 8.

Proof *(of Property 14)*. To prove Property 14, we need to use Lemma 3 and Lemma 4. The first three assumptions of Property 14 and Lemma 4 are the same. Basically, Lemma 4 states that by having the first three assumptions of Property 14, if either inputs of neuron $N1$ are 1 at the time *time*, which is stated by the assumption $\left(Inputs[time] = 1 \vee Output(PL\_N2(PLP))[time] = 1\right)$, then $Output(N1)$ is 1 at the time $time + 1$, which is stated by $Output\left(PL\_N1(PLP)\right)[time + 1] = 1$. Using Property 7 and considering that $Inputs = (011)^*(\varepsilon + 0 + 01)$, which is the input to the series of n delayers, as reasoned just above, we can conclude that $Output(NSeries) = 0^n(011)^*(\varepsilon + 0 + 01)$. To express the time when $time > n$, we can write $time = n + m$ for $m > 1$. Note that $time$ is universally quantified in the statement of Lemma 4 and can be instantiated by any natural number. We instantiate it by $time = n + m - 1$, and based on the reasoning above, we know that $Output(NSeries) = 0^n(011)^*(\varepsilon + 0 + 01)$, which is the input of the positive loop in the series composition. Thus, we can conclude that when $((m - 1) \bmod 3) = 1$ or $((m - 1) \bmod 3) = 2$ (the remainder of $m - 1$ divided by 3 is either 1 or 2), then $Output(NSeries)[n + m - 1] = 1$. Note that we have $time = n + m - 1 < length(Output(N1))$ as one of the assumptions of Property 14, which is required in order to apply Lemma 4. Thus, by Lemma 4, we can conclude that when $time = n + m > n + 1$ and $[((m - 1) \bmod 3) = 1$ or $((m - 1) \bmod 3) = 2]$, it follows that $Output(N1)[n + m] = 1$. This means that $Output(N1)[time] = 1$ when $time = n + m > n + 1$ and $[(m \bmod 3) = 2$ or $(m \bmod 3) = 0]$. The only remaining case is to prove that $Output(N1)[time] = 1$ is also true when $time = n + m > n + 1$ and $(m \bmod 3) = 1$.

At this point, we need to use Lemma 3. Again, the first three assumptions of Property 14 and Lemma 3 are the same. Similarly, Lemma 3 states that by having the first three assumptions of Property 14, if the only input of neuron $N2$ in the positive loop is 1 at the time $time$, which is stated by the assumption $Output(PL\_N1(PLP))[time] = 1$, then $Output(N2)$ is 1 at the time $time + 1$, which is stated by $Output(PL\_N2(PLP))[time + 1] = 1$. Note that $time$ is also universally quantified in the statement of Lemma 3 and can be instantiated by any natural number. We instantiate it by $time = n + m - 2$, and by the above reasoning we know that $Output(N1)[time] = 1$ when $time = n + m > n + 1$ and $[(m \bmod 3) = 2$ or $(m \bmod 3) = 0]$. By replacing $n + m$ with $n + m - 2$ in this reasoning, we have $Output(N1)[n + m - 2] = 1$ when $n + m - 2 > n + 1$ and $[((m - 2) \bmod 3) = 2$ or $((m - 2) \bmod 3) = 0]$. Thus, by Lemma 3, and the facts that $Output(N1)[n + m - 2] = 1$ when $n + m - 2 > n + 1$ and $[((m - 2) \bmod 3) = 2$ or $((m - 2) \bmod 3) = 0]$, we can conclude that $Output(N2)[n + m - 1] = 1$ when $time = n + m - 2 > n + 1$ and $[((m - 2) \bmod 3) = 2$ or $((m - 2) \bmod 3) = 0]$. Note that we need $n + m - 1 < length(Output(N1))$ to be true to be able to apply Lemma 3 and because $Output(N1)[time] = 1$ when $time = n + m$, we can conclude that $n + m$ is a valid index and thus $n + m < length(Output(N1))$. We know that $length(Output(N1)) = length(Output(N2))$, and thus we can conclude that $n + m - 1 < n + m <$

$length(Output(N1)) = length(Output(N2))$. This means that $Output(N2)[time - 1] = 1$ when $time = n + m$, $n + m - 2 > n + 1$, and $[((m - 2) \bmod 3) = 2$ or $((m - 2) \bmod 3) = 0]$. By restating this conclusion, we have $Output(N2)[time - 1] = 1$ when $time = n + m > n + 3$ and $[((m - 1) \bmod 3) = 0$ or $((m - 1) \bmod 3) = 1]$.

We use Lemma 4 again but this time with $Output(N2)[time] = 1$ in the assumption $(Inputs[time] = 1 \lor Output(PL\_N2(PLP))[time] = 1)$. We know that $Output(N2)[time - 1] = 1$ when $time = n + m > n + 3$ and $[((m - 1) \bmod 3) = 0$ or $((m - 1) \bmod 3) = 1]$. By Lemma 4, we can conclude that $Output(N1)[time] = 1$ when $time = n + m > n + 3$ and $[((m - 1) \bmod 3) = 0$ or $((m - 1) \bmod 3) = 1]$. This means that $Output(N1)[time] = 1$ when $time = n + m > n + 3$ and $[(m \bmod 3) = 1$ or $(m \bmod 3) = 2]$. Let us put together the two results we have for $Output(N1)[time]$ when $time = n + m$.

$time = n + m > n + 1$ and $[(m \bmod 3) = 2$ or $(m \bmod 3) = 0] \Longrightarrow Output(N1)[time] = 1$.

$time = n + m > n + 3$ and $[(m \bmod 3) = 1$ or $(m \bmod 3) = 2] \Longrightarrow Output(N1)[time] = 1$.

We can simplify the assumptions of the second one and just keep the one we need and rewrite these two results as follows:

$time = n + m > n + 1$ and $[(m \bmod 3) = 2$ or $(m \bmod 3) = 0] \Longrightarrow Output(N1)[time] = 1$.

$time = n + m > n + 3$ and $(m \bmod 3) = 1 \Longrightarrow Output(N1)[time] = 1$.

We know that $m = 2$ implies $(m \bmod 3) = 2$ and $m = 3$ implies $(m \bmod 3) = 0$, which means they are covered by the first case. Therefore, we can mix these two and unify the result as follows:

$time = n + m > n + 1 \Longrightarrow Output(N1)[time] = 1$.

This completes the proof.

Similar to Property 9, we have a property here that is focused on the output of the neuron $N2$ stating that this neuron starts emitting spikes with one more delay in comparison to $N1$. This property is expressed as follows:

Property 15. $\forall$ *(Inputs: list nat)*

$$\big(NSeries\!:(NeuronSeries\ Inputs)\big)$$

$$\Big(PLP\!:\big(PositiveLoop\ (NSOutput(NSeries))\big)\Big)\ (time\!:nat),$$

$$w_1\big(PL\_N1(PLP)\big) \geq \tau\big(PL\_N1(PLP)\big) \wedge w_2\big(PL\_N1(PLP)\big) \geq \tau\big(PL\_N1(PLP)\big) \wedge$$

$$w_1\big(PL\_N2(PLP)\big) \geq \tau\big(PL\_N2(PLP)\big) \wedge Inputs = (011)^*(\varepsilon + 0 + 01) \wedge$$

$$length\big(NeuronList(NSeries)\big) = n \wedge n + 2 < time \wedge$$

$$\begin{pmatrix} \forall i\ 0 \leq i < n, \quad length\big(w(NeuronList(NSeries)[i])\big) = 1 \wedge \\ w_1(NeuronList(NSeries)[i]) > \tau(NeuronList(NSeries)[i]) \end{pmatrix} \wedge$$

$$time < length\big(Output(PL\_N2(PLP))\big) \rightarrow Output(PL\_N2(PLP))[time] = 1$$

Property 15 has almost the same assumptions as Property 14 except for $n + 2 < time$, which expresses one unit of time longer delay for producing 1s in the output of $N2$. Also, $time < length\big(Output(PL\_N2(PLP))\big)$ ensures that the index to $Output(N2)$ is in range. Like the proof of Property 9, which was a direct corollary of Property 8, this property is a direct corollary of Property 14.

Proof *(of Property 15).* We know that since $time > n + 2$ it is also the case that $time > n + 1$. Again, to express the time when $time > n + 2$, we can write $time = n + m$ for $m > 2$. Also, because $Output(N1)$ has the same length as $Output(N2)$, we can conclude that $time = n + m < length\big(Output(PL\_N2(PLP))\big)$ implies $time = n + m < length\big(Output(PL\_N1(PLP))\big)$. This means we can use Property 14 and conclude that for $time = n + m > n + 1$, $Output(N1)[time] = 1$. Now, since we have the first three assumptions of Lemma 3 because they are the same as the first three assumptions of this property, if we instantiate $time$ in the statement of Lemma 3 with $n + m - 1$, we can conclude that $Output(N2)[n + m] = 1$ when $n + m - 1 > n + 1$ and $Output(N1)[n + m - 1] = 1$. Note that $time = n + m > n + 2$ implies that $n + m - 1 > n + 1$. Thus, we can conclude that when $time = n + m > n + 2$, $Output(N2)[time] = 1$. This completes the proof.

7.4 Coq Implementation

In this section, we present the definition of properties stated in the previous section in Coq. As mentioned earlier, a big advantage for the series composition is that we do not need a new record definition because archetypes are like black boxes in this composition and we can just replace the input of one with the output of the other one. That is why we can state the properties directly. The statement of Property 14 is shown in Figure 59. This property is called `SeriesN_PositiveLoop_Composition1` in Coq.

```
Theorem SeriesN_PositiveLoop_Composition1:
  forall (Inputs: list nat) (Series: @NeuronSeries Inputs)
         (PLP: @PositiveLoop (NSOutput Series)) (time: nat),
  AllDelayers (NeuronList Series) ->
  Pattern (rev Inputs) [0%nat;1%nat;1%nat] 0%nat ->
  Qle_bool (Tau (PL_N1 PLP)) (hd 0 (Weights (PL_N1 PLP)))  = true ->
  Qle_bool (Tau (PL_N1 PLP)) (hd 0 (tl (Weights (PL_N1 PLP))))  = true ->
  Qle_bool (Tau (PL_N2 PLP)) (hd 0 (Weights (PL_N2 PLP)))  = true ->
  (lt ((length (NeuronList Series)) + 1%nat)%nat time) ->
  (lt time (length (Output (PL_N1 PLP)))) ->
  List.nth time (rev (Output (PL_N1 PLP))) 0%nat = 1%nat.
```

Figure 59. Statement of the property `SeriesN_PositiveLoop_Composition1` (Property 14) in Coq

In Figure 59, `(Series: @NeuronSeries Inputs)` expresses that `Series` is a series of the single input neuron archetype defined in Figure 37 and `(PLP: @PositiveLoop (NSOutput Series))` expresses that the output of `Series`, expressed as `(NSOutput Series)` is the input of `PLP`, which is the positive loop in the series composition. Recall that `AllDelayers (NeuronList Series)` states that all neurons in `Series` are delayer neurons using the function `AllDelayers` defined in Figure 40. The rest of the assumptions are almost the same as the property `TwoPositiveLoopAmplifier1` (Property 8) shown in Figure 45 for the positive loop. The only difference is `(lt ((length (NeuronList Series)) + 1%nat)%nat time)` to express that $time > n + 1$, where n is the number of neurons in `Series`. The conclusion `List.nth time (rev (Output (PL_N1 PLP))) 0%nat = 1%nat` is the Coq representation of the conclusion of Property 14 namely, $Output(PL\_N1(PLP))[time] = 1$.

In Figure 60, the statement of Property 15 is expressed in Coq. This property is called `SeriesN_PositiveLoop_Composition2`. The only difference in the assumptions of this property from the assumptions of property `SeriesN_PositiveLoop_Composition1` is that `(lt ((length (NeuronList Series)) + 2%nat)%nat time)`, which shows that $time > n + 2$ because the neuron N2 starts producing one in its output after the time $n + 2$.

```
Theorem SeriesN_PositiveLoop_Composition2:
  forall (Inputs: list nat) (Series: @NeuronSeries Inputs)
         (PLP: @PositiveLoop (NSOutput Series)) (time: nat),
  AllDelayers (NeuronList Series) ->
  Pattern (rev Inputs) [0%nat;1%nat;1%nat] 0%nat ->
  Qle_bool (Tau (PL_N1 PLP)) (hd 0 (Weights (PL_N1 PLP)))  = true ->
  Qle_bool (Tau (PL_N1 PLP)) (hd 0 (tl (Weights (PL_N1 PLP))))  = true ->
  Qle_bool (Tau (PL_N2 PLP)) (hd 0 (Weights (PL_N2 PLP)))  = true ->
  (lt ((length (NeuronList Series)) + 2%nat)%nat time) ->
  (lt time (length (Output (PL_N2 PLP)))) ->
  List.nth time (rev (Output (PL_N2 PLP))) 0%nat = 1%nat.
```

Figure 60. Statement of the property `SeriesN_PositiveLoop_Composition2` (Property 15 in Coq

7.5 Other Possible Compositions

As can be seen, both series and nested coupling of archetypes give us a lot of options and different functionalities. Compositions are an area to explore in order to find useful functionalities for the human neural network. We do not explore the nested composition in this book. It is more difficult to explore the nested composition than the series composition because it depends on the internal structure of an archetype. In other words, we need to define a new record for every different nested coupling of archetypes. For example, consider the modification of Figure 57 where we place the new archetype between the output of N2 and the input of N1 instead. Certainly, we have a different structure and a different functionality. Another challenge with the nested composition is how to deal with time in the structure. For instance, if we replace the nested archetype in Figure 57 with the series of single input delayers, we should consider that the output of the neuron N1 experiences n (the number of neurons in the series of delayers delays before reaching the input of the neuron N2, while N2 sends its output directly to N1. Therefore, we need to define a new record with some constraints to express the way inputs and outputs of neurons and the nested archetypes are connected. We also need to define some functions which apply the inputs in the right order and at the right place in the internal structure of the outer archetype. Needless to say, the original record definition of the outer archetype cannot help in defining this new structure. All these challenges for the nested composition come from the fact that the outer archetype cannot be considered as a black box in this type of coupling. We need to customize its internal structure to embed the nested archetype. Defining a structure for nested archetypes in the model and proving properties about them is left as a future work but, as mentioned earlier, some properties about some nested compositions have been verified by model checkers in [20, 27], which gives us a place to start.

The series composition can also generate diverse functionalities. We only mentioned one sample of such a coupling in the previous section. Recall that the advantage of the series composition over the nested composition is that we do not need to create new record definitions, new constraints, and new functions for this coupling. We can just use the archetype definitions we have already defined and connect the output of one archetype to the input of the other one. For example, the series of delayer neurons can also delay the oscillation of 1100 in the output of the negative loop displayed in Table 2. We can also delay one of the inputs of the neurons in a contralateral inhibition in order to delay the output of the inhibited or activated neuron. We can also add more than two archetypes in a series composition. For example, by adding two series of delayers, we can delay both the inhibited and the activated neurons in a contralateral inhibition. Even switching the role of archetypes in the series composition can give us a different functionality. Although having the series of delayer neurons as a receiver of the output of the positive loop or the negative loop does not change the outcome of these compositions in this case, it could change it in other cases. We can also combine the positive loop or the negative loop with the contralateral inhibition. The area to be explored is vast and there are different functionalities that can be achieved using different couplings. Once we get a new composition, its output should be discussed with biologists to determine whether the obtained behavior is biologically relevant. Coupling archetypes for achieving desired functionalities is also an area of future work.

Chapter 8

Conclusion and Future Work

In this chapter, we summarize and provide the conclusion for this book. We also conclude with possible future work and ideas to follow up this book. There are two major parts for the future work. First, we enumerate what structures and properties in this model are left to be explored and proved, and also some ideas about their proofs. Second, we discuss the next step of this research toward a more comprehensive model of neural networks.

8.1 Summary and Conclusion

In this book, we built and verified a model for neuronal networks, which is a step toward generating a model with more aspects of larger human neural networks. To create such a model, we started with the most basic and the smallest unit of a human neural network and used the LI&F model to define neurons in our model. We used record structures in the Coq proof assistant to define neurons and their fields based on the LI&F model. We also used Coq functions to define associated functionalities with a neuron such as weighted sum of inputs, membrane potential, and output. Then, we moved one step further and used parameterized records in Coq to define archetypes such as the series of delayer neurons, the positive loop, the negative loop and the contralateral inhibition, which consist of more than one neuron. Archetypes are functional structures in the human neural network and the next smallest unit of human neural networks after neurons. They can do simple functions such as delaying, transferring, filtering, etc. neuronal signals. Finally, we introduced two possible ways of coupling archetypes to make more complicated functional structures. These two main couplings are the series compositions and the nested compositions. We explained how using different archetypes in these compositions can give rise to different functionalities. Recall that rhythmic motions such as walking, running, breathing, etc. are well-known examples of actions that are generated by compositions of archetypes in our neural network.

Surely, a model is defined by its structure, behavior and properties. These properties need to be stated and verified. By consulting biologists, we extracted some properties of single input neurons in our neural network such as the delayer effect, the filter effect, the inhibitor effect, the spike decreasing effect, etc. We defined and proved these properties mathematically and also verified them using the Coq proof assistant. Also, we proved the inhibitor effect mathematically for multiple input neurons. After this, we presented properties about archetypes. Each archetype has different properties when it is fed with different inputs. We introduced the delayer effect property in the series of delayers archetype and we proved that this archetype can produce a delay equal to the number of neurons in the series. We also defined two properties for the positive loop, the negative loop, and the contralateral inhibition archetypes. We proved mathematically and verified formally properties of the positive loop. Finally, we introduced and proved two properties of the series composition of the series of delayer neurons and the positive loop. We also discussed other possible compositions.

As for the conclusion of this book, we built a model that can be considered as a foundation of a more comprehensive model of neuronal networks and is a step toward building a model for a big part of the human neural network. The neuronal networks we model can be extended easily to other types of biological networks such as gene regulatory networks or protein-protein interaction networks.

Our model can also be extended easily. More properties about neurons can be defined and proved without modifying the implementation of the structure of the neuron in Coq. Also, we can generate more archetypes with different structures and constraints using parameterized records in Coq. In Chapter 7, we also mentioned that the series composition can be studied and analyzed without defining a new record. We can just use the definitions of archetypes directly in stating a new property and define the connections between these archetypes in the series compositions. Although the nested compositions are more complicated and we need to define a new record for each of them, it is still extendable just by adding a new definition for a nested composition, where defined archetypes can be used in its fields. We will explain later an idea for including the nested compositions in an easier way. Needless to say, new properties in this model can be defined and proved using the previously defined and verified properties.

The other main contribution of this model is using theorem provers instead of model checkers. Although model checkers are more automatic and can provide a counter example when they fail to verify a property, they lack generality. On the other hand, theorem provers can prove properties for any input values, any length of input, and any amount of time. The main disadvantage of theorem provers is that they are not automatic and they need an expert to guide the proofs. In the next section, we explain a new direction of research that can combine advantages of both model checkers and theorem provers.

Although our model is focused on human neuronal networks, which is a step toward a model for bigger human neural networks as mentioned earlier, this model can be used for other types of networks such as regulatory, metabolic, and environmental networks. Also using our model, there is a potential that we can detect weakly active or inactive zones of the brain and come up with a treatment for mental disorders as we explained in Section 5.5 in more detail.

8.2 Future Work

There are several aspects of human neural networks that are not still known to biologists. Knowing that this magnificent structure that controls the human body is still not quite known leads us to conclude that no model can simulate all functions, behaviors, and properties of these networks, but this does not mean that a model cannot simulate a specific human neural network in a reasonable way. We designed a model for neuronal networks that is a step toward having a comprehensive model of the human neural network using the Coq proof assistant.

We proved some important properties about single input neurons in Chapter 5, but we only proved one property about multiple input neurons. As mentioned earlier, mathematical proofs are easier than verification of them in a proof assistant. We proved the inhibitor effect for multiple input neurons mathematically but we left the verification part in Coq as a future work. The mathematical proof of the inhibitor effect gives us a strong idea for its verification. We just need to do an induction on the number of time steps and use some `unfold` tactics for functions involved for defining this property. By simplifying the result, it can lead us to the conclusion of this property.

The other properties that we left for future work are the general versions of Property 8 and Property 9 about the positive loop. We did not state the general versions of these properties mathematically but we explained that the positive loop can have more than two neurons where each one activates the next, and the last one activates the first neuron. We claimed that when the input to the first neuron, which is also the input to the positive loop archetype, follows the pattern $(011)^*$, the first neuron starts emitting spikes after time 2 and each other neuron starts firing spikes by one unit of time delay in comparison to the neuron that activates it. The idea for the proof of the general versions of Property 8 and Property 9 is to use an induction on the number of neurons in the general version of the positive loop. The base case is the positive loop with only two neurons and thanks to the proofs of Property 8 and Property 9, we have already verified this case. We need to assume that these properties are true for $n - 1$ neurons for $n > 3$ and prove that they are true for n neurons. This can be done by proving that the output of the last neuron is 1 after time n, considering that its input is the output of the $n - 1$-th neuron in the positive loop structure of $n - 1$ neurons.

We also introduced two oscillation properties about the negative loop archetype when its input is a persistent sequence of 1s. These properties are stated as Property 10 and Property 11. Their conclusions express that neuron $N1$ follows the pattern 1100 starting at time 1 and neuron $N2$ follows the same starting at time 2 as shown in Table 2. To express these statements in Coq, we can use the Pattern function in Figure 46 that we have already defined. In order to prove these properties, we would need to prove some lemmas for these properties. An important lemma is showing that the output of neuron $N1$ at time $time + 1$ is 0, namely $Output(N1)[time + 1] = 0$, whenever both inputs of $N1$ at the time $time$ are 1, namely from $Inputs[time] = 1$ and $Output(N2)[time] = 1$. Also, we need another lemma that expresses that the output of neuron $N1$ at time $time + 1$ is 1 when $Inputs[time] = 1$ and $Output(N2)[time] = 0$. Note that the other combinations of inputs for neuron $N1$, namely when $Inputs[time] = 0$ and $Output(N2)[time] = 1$ or when $Inputs[time] = 0$ and $Output(N2)[time] = 0$, do not happen because $Input = 1^*$. We also need a lemma similar to Lemma 3 for the negative loop, which proves that $Output(N1)[time] = 1$ implies that $Output(N2)[time + 1] = 1$. Using these lemmas and considering four cases, which expresses all possible remainders of $time$ when it is divided by four, we can prove Property 10 and Property 11 for the negative loop.

We also stated two properties about the contralateral inhibition archetype when both inputs of this archetype, namely $Input1$ and $Input2$ are persistent sequences of 1s. These properties are stated as Property 12 and Property 13. The situation created in these two properties is called the winner takes all. Their conclusions express that neuron $N1$ starts producing 0 in its output starting at time 2 and neuron $N2$ starts producing 1 at time 1 as shown in Table 3, which mean neuron $N1$ is the winner and neuron $N2$ is the loser in these properties. Similar to properties 10 and 11 for the negative loop, we need some supporting lemmas. We need to prove a lemma that states when both inputs of neuron $N1$ are 1 at the time $time$, namely $Input1[time] = 1$ and $Output(N2)[time] = 1$, this neuron produces 0 in its output at the time $time + 1$, which means $Output(N1)[time + 1] = 0$. We also need to prove another lemma that states $Input2[time] = 1$ and $Output(N1)[time] = 0$ implies $Output(N2)[time + 1] = 1$. Note that we need to focus only on these combinations of inputs for these neurons to prove Property 12 and Property 13. In fact, by combining the results of the lemmas stated above, we can complete the proof of these properties, which express the situation of winner takes all in the contralateral inhibition archetype.

We discussed proofs and extensions that we already have in hand for our model but the more important question is what the next step of this research is. We proved some important properties about single input neurons. Although these properties make clear statements about possible tasks that neurons are capable of, such as delaying, filtering, and transferring signals, we know that single input neurons do not exist in the human neural network. Thus, we need to focus on more realistic properties about multiple input neurons. One possible direction of future work is to consult with biologist to extract interesting properties about multiple input neurons. As stated, we have proved the inhibitor effect for multiple input neurons. We have also explained in Section 5.3 how neurons with this property can generate a disability and lead us to detect weakly active or inactive zones of the brain.

Also, we can consider more complicated archetypes and prove important properties about them. We explained above how the positive loop can be extended to a general version of this archetype and the ideas of proving similar properties to Property 8 and Property 9 for the general version. Other archetypes can be extended as well and have a more general or more complicated version that simulate more realistic functions in the human neural network. We can also consult with biologists to define more archetypes and prove properties about them. There are still a lot of small functional units that can be explored. The long-term goal is to prove that whatever networks are, even big and complicated ones, can be expressed as a composition of archetypes. The idea is that when we compose two archetypes, either we get a neuronal network whose behaviour has a relevant biological meaning or not. If it has no biological meaning, we throw it away. Otherwise, either it is equivalent to an archetype has already been found (and we have to prove the equivalence), or it means we have found a new archetype.

We already explained that we can try different compositions of archetypes to achieve different functionalities. Our model is already strong enough for expressing more series compositions of archetypes. In other words, we can easily define more properties about different series compositions without defining a new structure. We explained in Chapter 7, that for the nested compositions we need a new definition for each possible coupling, which can be tedious. A possible direction of future work is to define an abstract structure that can be used to create a nested composition given the outer and the nested archetypes. We also need to define a way to receive the placement of the nested archetype into the outer archetype as an input to this abstract structure. Having such a structure can greatly facilitate the definition of new nested compositions and stating properties about them.

An interesting question here is how many new archetypes and corresponding properties we need to model, define and prove. Also, how many different compositions should be enough to have a complete set to model a big part of the human neural network. According to biologists, we are not very far from this set. To use the analogy of words, a few syllables allow us to build thousands of currently used words and a quasi-infinity of sentences. Moreover, beyond a certain number of neurons and a certain level of connectivity, other functional processes different from archetypes should emerge, like cell assemblies. Thus, the composition process should stop after a finite and limited (compared to the size of the brain number of iterations. Therefore, we should rapidly reach a point where we can fall back on already studied behaviors, expressed through various instances of neuronal networks, reducible to few neuronal archetypes and their compositions.

Finally, we can consider a hybrid method that combines advantages of both model checkers and theorem provers. We discussed the trade off between automation of model checkers and generality of theorem provers. To improve the verification process and increase the level of generality of properties, we can first use model checkers to filter properties. Those properties for which model checkers find a counter example do not hold and need not be considered further. Those that model checkers verify for some cases should be passed to theorem provers to be proved in a more general form. As can be seen, the area of verification of biological networks is very large and there are still many fields and cases that need further exploration. This book suggested a model for some structures in the neuronal network and is a step toward creating a more comprehensive model for larger human neural networks.

References

[1] Abdpvtltd diagrams, http://abdpvtltd.com/neuron-diagram-labeled/neuron-diagram-labeled-new-chapter-28-concept-28-2/

[2] Alur R., Belta C., Ivanicic F., Kumar V., Mintz M., Pappas G.J., Rubin H., Schug J., Hybrid modeling and simulation of biomolecular networks. *In: Springer-Verlag (ed.) In Proceedings of the 4th International Workshop on Hybrid Systems: Computation and Control (HSCC'01)*, LNCS, vol. 2034, pp. 19-32, March 2001.

[3] Aman B. and Ciobanu G., Modelling and verification of weighted spiking neural systems. *Theoretical Computer Science* 623, pp. 92-102, April 2016.

[4] Andrei O., Fernández M., Kirchner H., Pinaud B., Strategy-Driven Exploration for Rule-Based Models of Biochemical Systems with Porgy. *In: Hlavacek W. (eds) Modeling Biomolecular Site Dynamics. Methods in Molecular Biology*, vol 1945, pp. 43-70, Humana Press, New York, NY, April 2019.

[5] Bahrami A., De Maria, E., Felty A.P., Modelling and Verifying Dynamic Properties of Biological Neural Networks in Coq, *In Proceedings of the 9th International Conference on Computational Systems-Biology and Bioinformatics (CSBio 2018)*, ACM, Article No.: 12, pp 1-11, December 2018.

[6] Bernot G., Cassez F., Comet J., Delaplace F., Muller C., Roux O., Semantics of Biological Regulatory Networks, Electronic notes in Theoretical Computer Science, Vol 18, Issue 3, pp. 3-14, July 2007.

[7] Bernot G., Comet J., Richard A., Guespin J., Application of formal methods to biological regulatory networks: extending Thomas' asynchronous logical approach with temporal logic, *Journal of Theoretical Biology*, Vol 229, Issue 3, pp. 339-347, August 2004.

[8] Bertot Y. and Castéran P., Interactive Theorem Proving and Program Development - Coq'Art: The Calculus of Inductive Constructions, Texts in Theoretical Computer Science, An EATCS Series, Springer, 2004.

[9] Blinov M.L., Faeder J.R., Goldstein B., Hlavacek W.S., Bionetgen: software for rule-based modeling of signal transduction based on the interactions of molecular domains. *Bioinformatics*, Vol 20, Issue 17, pp. 3289–3291, June 2004.

[10] Chabrier-Rivier N., Chiaverini M., Danos V., Fages F., Schächter V., Modeling and querying biochemical interaction networks. *Theoretical Computer Science*, Vol 325, Issue 1, pp. 25-44, September 2004.

[11] Chaudhuri K. and Despeyroux J., A Hybrid Linear Logic for Constrained Transition Systems with Applications to Molecular Biology, *19th International Conference on Types for Proofs and Programs (TYPES 2013)*, July 2014.

[12] Cimatti A., Clarke E.M., Giunchiglia F., Roveri M., Nusmv: A new symbolic model verifier. *In: Proceedings of the 11th Intl. Conference on Computer Aided Verification*, CAV '99, pp. 495-499, Springer-Verlag, London, UK, July 1999.

[13] Clarke E.M., Grumberg O., Peleg D., *Model checking*. MIT Press, Cambridge, MA, USA, 1999.

[14] Constable R.L, Allen S.F., Bromley H.M., Cleaveland W.R., Cremer J.F., Harper R.W., Howe D.J., Knoblock T.B., Mendler N.P., Panangadem P., Sasaki J.T., Smith S.F., Implementing Mathematics with the Nuprl Proof Development System, Prentice Hall, October 1995.

[15] Coq reference manual. Retrieved from https://coq.inria.fr/distrib/current/-refman/index.html.

[16] Coquand T. and Huet G., The calculus of constructions, *Information and Computation*, 76, pp. 95-120, February 1988.

[17] Cybenko, G., Approximation by superpositions of a sigmoidal function. *Mathematics of Control, Signals and Systems*, Vol 2, Issue 4, pp. 303-314, December 1992.

[18] Danos V. and Laneve C., Formal molecular biology, *Theoretical Computer Science* 325(1), pp. 69-110, September 2004.

[19] De Maria E., Formal Methods for Systems Biology: Contributions. Habilitation à Diriger des Recherches. University of Côted'Azur, Nice, France, June 2020.

[20] De Maria E., Bahrami A., L'Yvonnet T., Felty A.P., Gaffé D., Ressouche A., Grammont F., On the Use of Formal Methods to Model and Verify Neuronal Archetypes, *Frontiers of Computer Science*, November 2020.

[21] De Maria E., Despeyroux J., Felty A.P., A Logical Framework for Systems Biology, *1st International Conference on Formal Methods in Macro-Biology (FMMB '14)*, Springer LNCS 8738, pp. 136-155, September 2014.

[22] De Maria E., Despeyroux J., Felty A.P., Lio P., Olarte C., Bahrami A., Computational Logic for Systems Biology, Biomedicine, and Neuroscience. Accepted for publication as a chapter in an "ISTE-Wiley" book, 2020.

[23] De Maria E. and Di Giusto C., Parameter Learning for Spiking Neural Networks Modelled as Timed Automata. *The 9th International Conference on Bioinformatics Models, Methods and Algorithms (BIOINFORMATICS '18)*, pp. 17-28, January 2018.

[24] De Maria E., Fages F., Rizk A., Soliman S., Design, optimization and predictions of a coupled model of the cell cycle, circadian clock, DNA repair system, irinotecan metabolism and exposure control under temporal logic constraints, *Theoretical Computer Science*, Vol 412, Issue 21, pp. 2108-2127, May 2011.

[25] De Maria E., Gaffé D., Girard Riboulleau C., Ressouche A., A Model-checking Approach to Reduce Spiking Neural Networks, *The 9th International Conference on Bioinformatics Models, Methods and Algorithms (BIOINFORMATICS '18)*, pp. 89-96, January 2018.

[26] De Maria E., Muzy A., Gaffé D., Ressouche A., Grammont F., Verification of Temporal Properties of Neuronal Archetypes Modeled as Synchronous Reactive Systems., Cinquemani E. and Donzé A., (Eds.), *In Hybrid Systems Biology - 5th International Workshop, (HSB '16)*, pp. 97–112, Grenoble, France, October 2016.

[27] De Maria E., L'Yvonnet T., Gaffé D., Ressouche A., Grammont F., Modelling and Formal Verification of Neuronal Archetypes Coupling, *The 8th International Conference on Computational Systems-Biology and Bioinformatics (CSBio 2017)*, pp. 3-10, December 2017.

[28] Dénès, M., Lesage B., Bertot Y., Richard A., Formal Proof of Theorems on Genetic Regulatory Networks, *The 11th International Symposium on Symbolic and Numeric Algorithms for Scientific Computing*, pp. 68-76, September 2009.

[29] Faeder J. and Gupta S., Introduction to rule-based modeling with BioNetGen and RuleBender, *The 11th q-bio Conference*, Rutgers University, July 2017.

[30] Fages F., Soliman S., Chabrier-Rivier N., Modelling and querying interaction networks in the biochemical abstract machine BIOCHAM, *Journal of Biological Physics and Chemistry*, Vol 4, Issue 2, pp. 64–73, 2004.

[31] Fages F., Floch F.M., Gay S., Jovanovska D., Rizk A., Soliman S., Traynard P., BIOCHAM 3.7.3 Reference Manual, Institut National de Recherche en Informatique et Automatique EPI Lifeware, Inria Paris-Rocquencourt, France, September 2015.

[32] Fernandez M., Kirchner H., Pinaud B., Strategic port graph rewriting: an interactive modelling framework, *Mathematical Structures in Computer Science*, Vol 29, Issue 5, pp. 615-662, University of Cambridge Press, May 2019.

[33] Fernandez M., Kirchner H., Pinaud B., Vallet J., Labelled graph strategic rewriting for social networks, *Journal of Logical and Algebraic Methods in Programming*, Vol 96, pp. 12-40, April 2018.

[34] Fontaine P., editor. *Proceedings of the 27th International Conference on Automated Deduction*, volume 11716 of Lecture Notes in Computer Science, Springer, August 2019.

[35] Fornito A., Zalesky A., Breakspear M., Graph analysis of the human connectome: Promise, progress and pitfalls. NeuroImage, Mapping the Connectome, Vol 80, pp. 426–444, October 2013.

[36] Garg A., Di Cara A., Xenarios I., Mendoza L., De Micheli G., Synchronous vs. Asynchronous Modeling of Gene Regulatory Networks, *Bioinformatics*, Vol 24, Issue 17, pp. 1917-1925, September 2008.

[37] Gerstner W. and Kistler W., Spiking Neuron Models: An Introduction, Cambridge University Press, New York, NY, USA, 2002.

[38] Girard Y., Linear Logic, *Theoretical Computer Science*, Vol 50, Issue 1, pp. 1-101, 1987.

[39] Gilbert D.R. and Heiner M., Advances in computational methods in systems biology. *Theoretical Computer Science*, Vol 599, pp. 2-3, September 2015.

[40] Gonthier G., Asperti A., Avigad J., Bertot Y., Cohen C., Garillot F., Le Roux S., Mahboubi A., O'Connor R., Ould BihaIoana S., Pasca I., Rideau L., Solovyev A., Tassi E., Théry L., A machine-checked proof of the odd order theorem, *In Proceedings of the 4th International Conference on Interactive Theorem Proving*, pp. 163–179. Springer, July 2013.

[41] Grammont F., Personal Interview, August 2018.

[42] Hagen G. and Tinelli C., Scaling up the formal verification of Lustre programs with SMT-based techniques. *Proceedings of the 2008 International Conference on Formal Methods in Computer-Aided Design (FMCAD '08)*, pp. 1–9, November 2008.

[43] Hales T., Adams M., Bauer G., Dang T.D., Harrison J., Hoang L.T., Kaliszyk C., Magron V., McLaughlin S., Nguyen T.T., Nguyen Q.T., Nipkow T., Obua S., Pleso J., Rute J., Solovyev A., Anta T.H., Tran N.T, Trieu T.D., Urban J., Vu K., Zumkeller R., A formal proof of the Kepler conjecture. *Forum of Mathematics, Pi*, Vol 5, May 2017.

[44] Halbwachs, N., Raymond, P.: Validation of synchronous reactive systems: from formal verification to automatic testing. *In: Asian Computing Science Conference (ASIAN'99)*, LNCS 1742, Springer Verlag, Phuket, Thailand, December 1999.

[45] Harrison J., O'Leary J., Tolmach A., editors. *Proceedings of the 10th International Conference on Interactive Theorem Proving*, Vol 141 of LIPIcs. Schloss Dagstuhl - Leibniz-Zentrum für Informatik, September 2019.

[46] Hecker M., Lambeck S., Toepfer S., Someren E., Guthke R., Gene regulatory network inference: Data integration in dynamic models-A review, *Biosystems*, Vol 96, Issue 1, pp. 86-103, April 2009.

[47] Hofestädt R. and Thelen S., Quantitative modeling of biochemical networks, *In Silico Biology*, IOS Press, vol. 1, pp. 39-53, 1998.

[48] Hucka M., Hoops S., Keating S.M., Le Nov`ere N., Sahle S., Wilkinson D.J., Systems Biology Markup Language (SBML) Level 2: Structures and Facilities for Model Definitions, SMBL Level 2 Version 4 Release 1, December 2008.

[49] Izhikevich E.M., Which model to use for cortical spiking neurons? *IEEE Transactions on Neural Networks*, Vol 15, Issue 5, pp. 1063–1070, September 2004.

[50] Kohn K.W., Molecular interaction map of mammalian cell cycle control and DNA repair systems, *Molecular Biology of the Cell*, Vol 10, Issue 8, pp. 2703-2734, August 1999.

[51] Kwiatkowska M., Norman G., Parker D., PRISM 4.0 2001 Verification of probabilistic real-time systems, Gopalakrishnan G. and Qadeer S., editors, *In Proceeding. 23rd International Conference on Computer Aided Verification (CAV'11)*, Springer, volume 6806 of LNCS, pp. 585-591, July 2011.

[52] Lapicque L., Recherches quantitatives sur l'excitation electrique des nerfs traitee comme une polarization. J Physiol Pathol Gen 9, pp. 620–635, 1907.

[53] Lathrop J.L., Lutz J.H., Lutz R.R., Potter H.D., Riley M.R., Population-Induced phase transitions and the verification of chemical reaction networks, 26th International Conference on DNA Computing and Molecular Programming (DNA 26), June 2020.

[54] Leeuwen J., Handbook of Theoretical Computer Science (Vol. B): Formal Models and Semantics, (Ed.) 1991, Chapter 16 Temporal and Modal Logic, MIT Press, Cambridge, MA, USA, 1991.

[55] Leroy X, Blazey S., Dargaye Z., Jourdan J., Schmidt M., Schommer B., Tristan J., The CompCert project. Compilers you can formally trust. http://compcert.inria.fr/.

[56] Klein G., Elphinstone K., Heiser G., Andronick J., Cock D., Derrin P., Elkaduwe D., Engelhardt K., Kolanski R., Norrish M., Sewell T., Tuch H., Winwood S., Sel4: Formal verification of an OS kernel. *In Proceedings of the ACM SIGOPS 22nd Symposium on Operating Systems Principles*, pp. 207-220, October 2009.

[57] Maass W., Networks of spiking neurons: The third generation of neural network models. *Neural Networks*, Vol 10. Issuer 9, pp. 1659–1671, December 1997.

[58] Maler O. and Batt G., Approximating continuous systems by timed automata. *In Proceedings Formal Methods in Systems Biology, First International Workshop (FMSB 2008)*, pp. 77–89, Cambridge, UK, June 2008.

[59] Markram H., The blue brain project. *Nat Rev Neurosci*, Vol 7, Issuer 2, pp. 153–160, February 2006.

[60] Matsuoka K., Mechanisms of frequency and pattern control in the neural rhythm generators, *Biological cybernetics*, Vol 56, Issue 5 and 6, pp. 345–353, July 1987.

[61] McCulloch, W. S., Pitts, W., A logical calculus of the ideas immanent in nervous activity. *The Bulletin of Mathematical Biophysics*, Vol 5, Issue 4, pp. 115-133, December 1943.

[62] Miller, D., Nadathur, G., Programming with Higher-Order Logic. Cambridge University Press, 2012.

[63] Minsky, M., Papert, S., Perceptrons: An Introduction to Computational Geometry, MIT Press, 1969.

[64] Nipkow T., Wenzel M., Paulson L.C., Isabelle/HOL: A Proof Assistant for Higher-orderLogic. Springer-Verlag, Berlin, Heidelberg, 2002.

[65] Owre S., Rajan S., Rushby J.M., Shankar N., Srivas M.K., PVS: Combining specification, proof checking, and model checking. Alur R. and Henzinger T.A., editors, *In Computer-Aided Verification (CAV'96)*, Vol 1102 of Lecture Notes in Computer Science, pp. 411–414, New Brunswick, NJ, Springer-Verlag, July 1996..

[66] Paugam-Moisy H. and Bohte S.M., Computing with spiking neuron networks. *In Handbook of Natural Computing*, pp. 335-376, 2012.

[67] Phillips A. and Cardelli L., A correct abstract machine for the stochastic pi-calculus. *Proceedings of BioConcur*, Electronic Notes in Computer Science, January 2004.

[68] Purves D., Augustine G.J., Fitzpatrick D., Hall W.C., Lamantia A.S., McNamara J.O., Williams S.M., (Eds.), Neuroscience (3rd ed.), Sinauer Associates, Inc, 2006.

[69] Rashid A., Hasan O., Siddique U., Tahar S., Formal reasoning about systems biology using theorem proving. *PLoS ONE*, Vol 12, Issue 7, e0180179, July 2017.

[70] Reddy V.N., Mavrovouniotis M.L., Liebman M.N., Petri net representations in metabolic pathways. *In: Proceedings of the 1st Intl. Conference on Intelligent Systems for Molecular Biology (ISMB '93)*, pp. 328-336. AAAI Press, July 1993.

[71] Regev A., Panina E.M., Silverman W., Cardelli L., Shapiro E., Bioambients: An abstraction for biological compartments, *Theoretical Computer Science*, Vol 325, Issue 1, pp. 141-167, September 2004.

[72] Regev A., Silverman W., Shapiro E.Y., Representation and simulation of biochemical processes using the pi-calculus process algebra, *In: Proceedings of the 6th Pacific Symposium of Biocomputing (PSB '01)*, pp. 459-470, January 2001.

[73] Richard A., Comet J.P., Bernot G., Graph-based modeling of biological regulatory networks: Introduction of singular states. *International Conference on Computational Methods in Systems Biology (CMSB '04)*, pp. 58-72, May 2004.

[74] Rougny A., Tour´e V., Moodie S., Balaur I., Czauderna T., Borlinghaus H., Dogrusoz U., Mazein A., Dr¨ager A., Blinov M.L., Vill´eger A., Haw R., Demir E., Mi H., Sorokin A., Schreiber F., Luna A., Systems Biology Graphical Notation: Process Description language Level 1, Version 2.0, May 2019.

[75] Sharangpani H.P. and Barton M. L., Statistical Analysis of Floating Point Flaw in the Pentium Processor, Technical Report, Intel Corporation, http://users.minet.uni-jena.de/~nez/rechnerarithmetik_5/fdiv_bug/intel_white11.-pdf, November 1994.

[76] Sporns O., The human connectome: Origins and challenges, *NeuroImage Special Issue: Mapping the Connectome*, Vol 80, pp. 53-61, October 2013.

[77] Sporns O., Structure and function of complex brain networks, *Dialogues in clinical neuroscience*, Vol 15, Issue 3, pp. 247-262, September 2013.

[78] Sporns O., Graph theory methods: applications in brain networks, *Dialogues in clinical neuroscience*, Vol 20, Issue 2, pp. 111-121, June 2018.

[79] Talcott C.L. and Knapp M., Explaining response to drugs using pathway logic, *The 15th International Conference on Computational Methods in Systems Biology (CMSB '17)*, pp. 249-264, September 2017.

[80] Thomas R., Boolean formalization of genetic control circuits, *Journal of Theoretical Biology*, Vol 42, Issue 3, pp. 563-585, December 1973.

[81] Thomas R., Regulatory networks seen as asynchronous automata: A logical description, *Journal of Theoretical Biology*, Vol 153, Issue 1, pp. 1-23, November 1991.

[82] Thomas R., Thieffry D., Kaufman M., Dynamical behavior of biological regulatory networks-i. Biological role of feedback loops and practical use of the concept of the loop-characteristic state. *Bulletin of Mathematical Biology*, Vol 57, Issue 2, pp. 247-276, March 1995.